SCHOLASTIC

Managing Independent Reading

Effective Classroom Routines

Lessons, Strategies, and
Literacy-Building Activities
That Teach Children the
Routines and Behaviors
They Need to Become
Better Readers

**by Deborah Diffily
and Charlotte Sassman**

NEW YORK • TORONTO • LONDON • AUCKLAND • SYDNEY
MEXICO CITY • NEW DELHI • HONG KONG • BUENOS AIRES

Teaching *Resources*

Acknowledgments

Ideas for books come to authors in many ways. Sometimes authors see a need or have particular expertise and contact an editor with the idea. Other times the editor suggests topics. Deborah and Charlotte acknowledge our editor Maria L. Chang, for helping us both ways. She has an uncanny ability to take our work and make it better. Maria, thanks for your guidance and support.

Our colleagues over the years deserve a thank-you as well. The support that teachers offer other teachers is invaluable. We feel fortunate to have worked with many great educators during our careers.

Cover design by Jason Robinson
Interior design by Jeffrey Dorman
Illustrations by James Hale and Rusty Fletcher

ISBN 0-439-59720-X
Copyright © 2005 by Deborah Diffily and Charlotte Sassman
All rights reserved.
Printed in the U.S.A.

4 5 6 7 8 9 10   40   18 17 16 15 14

Table of Contents

Chapter 1 — At the Beginning of the Year

Chapter 2 — For Emergent Readers

Chapter 3 — For Early Readers

Chapter 4 — For Independent Readers

Introduction

Across the country, thousands of early childhood educators gather young children together for their daily reading lesson. Teachers introduce new skills, reinforce skills not yet mastered by children, and support both struggling and excelling readers—all while infusing children with a love for reading. Day after day these teachers and their students participate in this amazing and critical ritual.

Regardless of what reading program early childhood classes use, children engage in certain routines and activities to ensure that the time for reading instruction is efficient. Since time is always an issue in elementary classes, teachers try to make every minute of instruction count. With routines set in place, all children know what behaviors are expected of them and the teacher does not have to repeatedly tell them what to do at different times during the language-arts block. When clear routines and behavioral expectations are established for group work, teachers spend less time waiting to start the lesson and are interrupted fewer times during lessons. When children know what activities are available to them during reading-choice time, they are less likely to interrupt the teacher's instruction to a small group of students.

Classroom Environment

For routines to be most effective, the classroom itself must support children as they work not only as a group, but also individually, with a partner, and in small groups. See the checklist for evaluating classroom arrangement on page 6.

Group Routines

Teaching children group routines and giving them opportunities to practice each routine make group experiences more time-efficient and enjoyable. A first-grade teacher expresses this practice as "looking at the big picture." That is, because she spends quite a bit of time at the beginning of the year helping children learn her routines, she does not have to repeat this instruction throughout the year. By "looking at the big picture," she teaches children to be more independent and holds them responsible for their learning.

When children are thoroughly familiar with the class routines, they come to the group area when they are asked to do so. They quietly find a place to sit. They do not argue with each other about who can and cannot see the book during read-aloud. Children do not wander around the class during Drop Everything and Read (DEAR) times. They know what is expected of them. They understand exactly what it means to listen to a partner, read the news of the day, or act out a story.

☑ Checklist for Evaluating Classroom Arrangement

☐ Are books easily accessible to all children?

☐ Can all children reach center materials easily?

☐ Are different types of writing utensils and paper easily accessible to all children?

☐ Are there different types of places children can choose to work in; for example, at a table, at a desk, on the floor at a table with shortened legs, in corners of the room, or in a private space?

☐ Are clipboards available for children who choose to sit on the floor?

☐ Is there a well-defined space where all children in the class can sit comfortably for group meetings?

☐ Are there several areas where small groups of children can work comfortably?

☐ Is an alphabet chart displayed prominently?

☐ Is a word wall displayed prominently?

☐ Are resources such as the alphabet chart and the word wall posted low enough so that children can reach them?

☐ Are "traffic lanes" established so children can move around the room without running into each other?

In classes where routines have not been established, children take longer to come together and the teacher has to wait for them to settle down before beginning to teach. In some early childhood classes, this can take up to ten minutes—a waste of valuable instructional time.

Invest time in the first few weeks of school teaching, modeling, and practicing these routines and activities so that during the rest of the year, you can spend more quality time teaching.

Individual Routines

When you are working with a small group of children, other students need to know what to do. Establish individual routines and activities to keep children engaged while you teach small groups. Just as reading instruction from a teacher is critically important, the work that children do individually or with a partner is equally important.

Reading experts know that young children learn from each other. As first-grader Krizz-Tina remarked: "You are supposed to help each other in school. You don't tell the answers, you just make your friend's brain think." Learning to read and write occurs when children talk about books or about their writing with other classmates. For children to learn the most they can from each other, you need to create learning experiences that keep them focused on reading and writing.

Teach, model, and practice specific routines to provide children with a variety of activities in which they can stay focused on reading and writing. When children know these routines and activities, they can work without adult support and get sustained independent practice in reading. This provides virtually uninterrupted blocks of time so you can focus on small groups of children without having to attend to the other students in the class.

There are many different approaches to consider when planning routines and activities for an individual child's learning. Some teachers make specific daily assignments based on the instruction that each child needs. Personalized or individualized contracts hold the child accountable for his or her daily assignments. Other teachers allow children to choose among any of the reading routines or activities previously taught to the class, while other teachers limit the activities by posting a menu of individual activities from which children may choose. Still others create a rotation schedule to provide every child in the

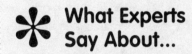

What Experts Say About...

Grouping Children for Reading Experiences

- Children who are put in the "bottom" group in first grade usually stay in the bottom group throughout elementary school.

- Children in the "bottom" group often become increasingly resistant to reading instruction.

- All too often, the highest-ability readers have more opportunities to read in school than other students. This is often referred to as the Matthew Effect.

- Reading groups should change. Children should not be expected to stay in the same groups throughout the year.

- Reading groups can be formed by characteristics other than reading ability. Temporary groups can be formed based on the topic that students will read about (books at several different levels must be identified).

Sources: Cunningham & Allington, 1994; Fountas & Pinnell, 1996; Juel, 1988; Stanovich, 1986

class an opportunity to participate in each activity during reading-choice time, self-selected activities, or literacy centers. It doesn't matter what you call this block of time or which approach you use to implement individual routines and activities. However, when considering whether to assign activities or to allow children to choose what they work on, research indicates that children tend to engage more deeply in activities that they choose for themselves.

Organization of the Book

The lessons in this book are organized into four broad chapters: beginning-of-the-year routines, strategies and routines for emergent readers, for early readers, and for independent readers.

The first chapter, "At the Beginning of the Year," contains strategies and routines that are typically taught in the first six to eight weeks of school. Many of these mini-lessons are procedural, setting up routines that guide what children do during different parts of their reading instruction. Children need to know exactly what behaviors are expected of them during different activities. The time invested in teaching and practicing both individual and group routines at the beginning of the year saves an incredible amount of time through the rest of the year.

The next three chapters are organized according to children's reading abilities. Chapter 2, "For Emergent Readers," applies to beginning kindergarten and first-grade students. The "For Early Readers" chapter is geared for late kindergarten to middle first grade. Finally, "For Independent Readers" is written for late first grade or second grade. These suggested grade-level spans take into account the wide range of abilities in each class. We encourage you to choose different routines from each section for different students in your class.

Lesson Organization

Following the overview that begins each chapter, you will find strategies for readers and suggested reading lessons or activities (divided into whole- and small-group activities as well as individual and partner activities) to teach children the routines and behaviors they need to become better readers.

The lessons, strategies, and literacy-building activities are organized into mini-lessons so busy teachers can easily teach needed routines and activities to the class. Each mini-lesson is coded with suggested times to teach that strategy, routine, or activity to children, depending on their grade level:

KF Kindergarten students in the fall
KW Kindergarten students in the winter
KS Kindergarten students in the spring
1F First-grade students in the fall
1W First-grade students in the winter
1S First-grade students in the spring
2F Second-grade students in the fall
2W Second-grade students in the winter
2S Second-grade students in the spring

Most mini-lessons have multiple codes. Many strategies and routines should be taught to all children at the beginning of the year. For example, all kindergarten, first-, and second-grade students need to learn behaviors expected of them during read-aloud and DEAR times, what being a serious reader looks like, and how to respond to literature. Even if children were previously in classrooms in which these routines were practiced, you should reteach this new grouping of children so that there are no questions about what behaviors are expected of them.

While each mini-lesson is coded, these codes are only suggestions for the time of year the routine or activity should be introduced to young children. Some classes will be ready sooner than others. You are in the best position to decide when your students are ready for each strategy, routine, and activity.

Each mini-lesson is divided into ten sections:

Lesson Target: The primary focus for the lesson

Why Teach This: The reason that this skill is important or how this particular lesson contributes to children's reading development

Secondary Objectives: Quite often, multiple concepts/skills are integrated into single lessons for young children. This section suggests one to three other objectives that can be met through each lesson.

Links to English Language Arts (ELA) Standards: One or more of the twelve International Reading Association/National Council of Teachers of English Standards for English Language Arts that connect to the lesson. The standards are abbreviated, stating only those parts of each standard most closely linked to the lesson.

Learning Materials: Materials you will need to gather prior to the lesson

Time Range: Approximate length of time for the lesson

Before You Start: What you need to create, gather, or arrange before the lesson begins

Students' Prior Experience: What children need to be familiar with before the lesson begins

To Do: The lesson with suggested teacher language

Supporting Children's Learning: Different ways to reinforce the main objective, including methods appropriate for kinesthetic learners, English-language learners, or struggling readers

These lessons are designed to support you as you plan reading instruction for kindergarten, first-, or second-grade children. Use them in the order given or choose appropriate lessons as needed. Teaching reading routines and activities in your program of balanced literacy ensures that the literacy instruction time is used as efficiently as possible. In classes where reading routines and activities are well-established, children learn to read and become better, independent readers.

CHAPTER ONE

At the Beginning of the Year

Overview

Routines should be taught to children from the first or second day of the school year. The sooner children learn the procedures and behaviors that make whole-group instruction and small-group learning experiences run smoothly, the more beneficial it is for everyone. They learn what to expect from the block of time dedicated to reading, and they soon know what is expected from them during this time. Teachers who establish routines at the beginning of the year spend much less time on classroom-management issues than teachers who do not.

The routines in this section focus on different types of learning experiences that are repeated many times throughout the year. For example, the first routine establishes what is expected of children during read-aloud times. Ideally, read-alouds should occur at least once a day, preferably more often. For children to benefit from these experiences, you need to explicitly explain to them what to do while you are reading to the whole class. For example, if you want children to sit cross-legged and flat on the floor, this must be described in detail. Just saying "sit and listen" is not enough. Young children need to know the specific details of what to do and have opportunities to practice this new behavior.

Be sure to write notes on chart paper while discussing a routine with children. Then lead the class in practicing those behaviors several times, so children clearly understand the expectations. After several practices, most children will remember the routine and follow those behaviors most of the time. There may be times when young children forget, or they get so excited about other issues that they cannot seem to do what they know they are supposed to do. When this occurs, find the chart paper with the notes from the original meeting and go through the steps of the routine one more time as a reminder for children.

Other mini-lessons establish children's behaviors for various whole-group learning experiences, such as group discussions and DEAR time. Individual routines help children learn what to do when they are expected to work on their own. These include tasks such as getting help from classmates when they cannot ask the teacher a question and checking out books to take home, as well as daily assignments, such as responding to literature.

Each mini-lesson in this section has the logo for kindergarten, first grade, and second grade. Even though beginning second-grade students have typically been in school for at least two years, they need to be taught what is expected of them in this particular classroom.

Teaching What Readers Do

KF **1F** **2F**

Establishing Behavioral Expectations for Read-Alouds

Lesson Target
To have children clearly understand the behaviors expected of them during a whole-group read-aloud

Why Teach This
By establishing class procedures early in the year, you ensure that all children understand the routines of the class. Additionally, many routines like this one are used throughout the school day. Thus, it is vitally important that all children understand these expectations.

Secondary Objective
• To reinforce behaviors for all large-group meetings

Links to ELA Standards
• Students read a wide range of print and nonprint texts to build an understanding of texts.
• Students participate as knowledgeable, reflective members of a variety of literacy communities.

Learning Materials
• book
• easel
• chart tablet
• basket with markers, self-adhesive notes, highlighting tape, and other supplies

Time Range
10–15 minutes

> **Teacher Tip**
> Keep teaching supplies in a basket or small plastic container to ensure that you have on hand what you need to support the lesson. Keep markers, wipe-off pens and eraser, self-adhesive notes, ruler, pens, pencils, transparent tape, highlighting tape, a small stapler, and other supplies near the group area for easy accessibility.

Before You Start
Decide where you want students to sit during read-alouds. Arrange the physical environment so that there is a sufficiently large area for all children to sit comfortably. (See diagram on page 12.) If the meeting area is too small, children are more likely to have problems (e.g., complaining about not having a place to sit, complaining about not being able to see the book, nudging each other, pushing their feet against someone else, and so on).

Define the meeting area with a carpet, rug, or tape on the floor, or create the boundaries by positioning bookshelves or other furniture in ways that help children

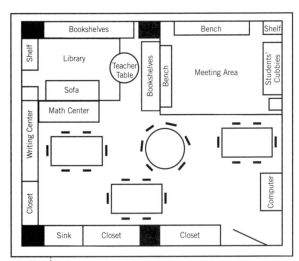

From *Classroom Management in Photographs* by Maria L. Chang

TEACHING STRATEGIES

Concepts of Print That Can Be Shared During Read-Alouds

- Front and back covers of the book
- Title, author, illustrator
- Title page
- Left-to-right directionality of print, return sweep
- Concept of letter, capital and lowercase letters
- Concept of word, first and last letters of a word
- Concept of sentence, first and last word in a sentence
- Matching one spoken word to one printed word
- Noting of space used between words

Other forms of print should be pointed out to children after most understand the common concepts of print. These include punctuation, chapter and/or title placement, and the line differences between prose and poetry.

understand where they are to sit during group meetings. Make sure that there are clear paths for students to come to the meeting area and to return to other parts of the classroom.

Arrange the area so that materials—such as a chart tablet, markers, self-adhesive notes, highlighting tape, and ruler—used during or following a read-aloud are readily accessible.

Students' Prior Experience

None

To Do

Call children to the group meeting area. Explain that you will be reading aloud a wonderful story to them and that this read-aloud activity is something that you will be doing every day. Say: *In order for everyone to enjoy the stories being read aloud, we will first discuss some of the things we need to do during read-aloud time.*

Hold up a book so that all children can see its illustrations.

> ### Teacher Tip
> Use the sample letter on page 13 to remind children's families about the importance of reading aloud to young children. When families understand what is going on in class, they are more likely to support your efforts at home.

Say: *Many of the books I will read have beautiful illustrations that I want everyone to see. If you cannot see the illustrations from your spot, you'll need to find a new place to sit. In our class, we are not going to tell other people to move. If you can't see, don't complain. Just move to a place where you can see.*

Ask children: *How can you show me that you are ready to listen to a story?* Write children's responses on chart paper. Guide children into listing behaviors such as:

1. Sit where you can see the book.
2. Sit flat on the floor.
3. Face the teacher.
4. Keep your hands and feet in your own space.

Explain that you are going to read the list of behaviors aloud and that you want each child to do that action as you read. Read the list and model each

Why Reading Aloud Is Important

Dear Families:

Every day at school, we set aside time to read at least one book aloud. I gather the children around me and read a book with as much expression as I can. One question you can always ask your child is, *What book did your teacher read to the class today?*

Read-alouds are an important part of our daily schedule because young children learn so much from being read to. They learn how good readers sound. From fiction, children learn that stories have a beginning, middle, and ending, and they learn about characters and settings. From nonfiction, they learn any number of facts about the world in which we live. Sometimes I use our read-aloud time to teach particular skills.

You don't have to actually teach specific skills to your children for them to benefit from a read-aloud experience at home. Just find some time every night to read a book to your child, then spend a few minutes talking about it.

Sincerely,

behavior. Explain that these are the expectations for read-alouds and that other behaviors may be added to the list as weeks go by.

After reading a short book, acknowledge that children have learned an important routine and remind them that everyone is expected to use these behaviors during group read-alouds.

Supporting Children's Learning

Not all children will remember the appropriate behaviors that have been discussed. It helps to practice each routine for several days in a row before expecting all children to remember. Still, some will forget. As a reminder, post the chart listing appropriate behaviors on the wall near the group meeting area. For those few children who need further reminders, ask them to draw a picture of what "read-aloud behavior" looks like. Post those drawings near the list.

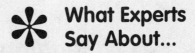

What Experts Say About...

The Importance of Reading Aloud to Young Children

- Listening to adults read to them helps children develop a love for books and reading.
- Reading aloud gives children access to books that are too difficult for them to read on their own.
- Reading aloud to children supports their vocabulary development.
- Reading aloud enriches children's background knowledge.
- Reading aloud from expository text shows children how information can be gained through reading.
- Reading with expression models fluency for children.
- Read-alouds introduce children to a variety of genres.

Sources: Burns, Griffin, & Snow, 1999; Cunningham & Allington, 1999; Fountas & Pinnell, 2001, Taberski, 2000

KF **1F** **2F**

Learning What Being a Serious Reader Looks Like

Lesson Target

To help children understand that reading is an endeavor that must be taken seriously

Why Teach This

Establishing clear expectations for every aspect of the reading-block time helps with classroom management as well as ensuring successful reading experiences. When children are engaged in productive work, they stay engaged for longer periods of time, increasing their learning.

Secondary Objectives
- To improve a variety of reading skills
- To keep children on task during reading times
- To reduce interruptions

Link to ELA Standards
- Students participate as knowledgeable members of a variety of literacy communities.

Learning Materials
- chart tablet
- markers

Time Range
10–15 minutes

Before You Start
Think through the procedures that will help reading time be more effective and more efficient. See "To Do" below for examples.

Students' Prior Experience
Children have been introduced to routines for group meetings.

To Do
Gather children in the group meeting area. Explain that different behaviors are expected of all of us when we are in different situations. For example, an adult's behavior is different at a baseball game than it is in a doctor's waiting room. Have children compare their behavior at recess or at lunch with their behavior in the classroom.

Ask children to think about what someone would see if they observed them being "serious readers." Encourage them to think about the different activities they do during the reading block, such as independent reading or partner reading. Write children's suggestions on chart paper. Some suggestions might include:
- Find a private place to sit.
- Sit still when reading a book.
- Talk in a quiet voice when working with a partner.
- Do not sit in front of the door—you might get hurt.
- Do not sit in front of the bookshelves—people need to get books.
- Do not play around.
- Do your job.
- Put things back where they belong.

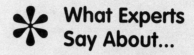

What Experts Say About...

The Amount of Time Children Spend Reading

- Teachers need to restructure the school day to make more time for reading, e.g., capture more academic time by reducing interruptions during the day, rethink the design of special programs, and make sure that children actually read during the time designated for reading instruction.
- On average, higher-achieving students read approximately three times as much each week as lower-achieving students.
- Children need to spend a minimum of 90 minutes every school day actually reading.
- Children need to spend at least 15 to 30 minutes every school day engaged in reading self-selected books.
- Struggling readers tend to spend less than one-third of reading instructional time actually reading. Two-thirds of their "reading" time is spent in skills drills, checking on vocabulary, and reviewing the story.

Sources: Allington, 2001; Allington & McGill-Franzen, 1989; Cunningham & Allington, 1994

If children do not mention one or more behaviors that you feel are important, use a pondering voice to say: *Do you think we should add* "talk in a quiet voice" *to our list?*

Post the final chart in the classroom and reread all suggestions. Emphasize that these are behaviors you expect from them when it's time to be "serious readers."

Supporting Children's Learning

When a child forgets—or is behaving in a way that is not consistent with the guidelines—ask him to meet you at the "Serious Readers" chart and read the appropriate guideline. Ask the child what kind of support he needs from you or his friends to help him remember that particular behavior.

Micah needed repeated reminders from his teacher to follow the class's guidelines about ending independent reading time. When Mrs. Brannon met with him privately, he said, "Sometimes I am just reading so hard that I don't hear you say it is time to clean up." They agreed that if Micah did not begin to put his things away after being asked the first time, then his friend Alvin would touch him on the shoulder to get his attention. Then he would begin to clean up "super fast." After repeating this behavior a few times, Micah began to recognize when it was time to stop reading and didn't need Alvin's help.

KF **1F** **2F**

Creating Behavioral Expectations for DEAR Time

Lesson Target

To clearly understand the behaviors expected during sustained silent reading (also called "Drop Everything and Read" or DEAR time)

Why Teach This

Self-selected reading is an important part of children's learning to read. DEAR time promotes children's love of reading because they are interacting with books of their own choice over a sustained period of time.

Secondary Objective

- To reinforce behaviors for all activities children will be expected to work on individually

Link to ELA Standards

- Students participate as knowledgeable members of a variety of literacy communities.

Learning Materials
• chart paper
• markers

Time Range
15–20 minutes

Before You Start
Consider the behaviors that will be expected of children during Drop Everything and Read. Some teachers insist that this is an individual activity and that children should not interact with each other during this time (just as in sustained silent reading). Other teachers believe that quiet interactions among children should be accepted if the children are discussing books. The lesson below gives suggestions for the first approach.

Students' Prior Experience
During silent reading time, remark on children's positive behaviors. For example, as you notice Jorge reading to himself, comment: *Jorge, you are working so hard at keeping your voice very low. Will you share that behavior with the class in our next meeting?* Continue this for at least a week before leading the conversation about behavioral expectations during DEAR time.

It would be helpful if students have had experience creating group rubrics before. Otherwise, explain rubrics during the second group meeting for this lesson.

To Do
Gather children in the group meeting area. Explain that reading is such an important thing that everyone in the class will participate in a special reading time called DEAR time. DEAR stands for "Drop Everything and Read." Explain to children that this will be a time when each person reads to himself or herself. Tell children how long this time will last, where they will go to select the books for DEAR time, and where they can sit or lie down during DEAR time.

Have DEAR time for one week, then hold a second meeting specifically to document the behaviors that will make DEAR time run most smoothly.

At the second meeting, comment that you have noticed that DEAR time has been going very well for some people but not so well for others. Ask students what behaviors they think makes DEAR time "good," and what behaviors make DEAR time "not so good." List children's answers on chart paper. After several comments about successes and concerns, suggest that these two lists could be used to make a rubric for checking their behavior at DEAR time. (If children are not familiar with rubrics, explain that a rubric is a chart used to judge behavior as "good" or "not so good." If the behavior is judged to be "not so good," the rubric offers suggestions to get the behavior into the "good" category.)

Divide a sheet of chart paper into two columns. Label the left column "Good DEAR Time" and the right column, "Not-So-Good DEAR Time." List positive behaviors under "Good DEAR Time." Write these positive behaviors directly from children's previous comments or reword them with their permission. Then develop corresponding statements for the "Not-So-Good DEAR Time" column. (See page 18.)

Reread the positive behaviors, then ask two or three children to act out what they should do during DEAR time. Ask other children to comment on the things they did right.

Supporting Children's Learning

When some children forget the DEAR time routine, walk over to those children and quietly remind them of the group discussion you had about DEAR time. Remind them of the behaviors that everyone agreed to. Alternatively, ask those children to meet you at the "Good/Not-So-Good DEAR Time" rubric. Point to the statement on the right column that they are doing. Slide your finger to the left and read the corresponding positive behavior, asking if they can do that. If several children seem to be having trouble remembering appropriate behaviors for DEAR time, have another group meeting where you read the rubric again. Have some of the children who do not remember the correct behaviors act out the positive behaviors as you read the "Good DEAR Time" side of the chart.

DEAR Time	
GOOD	**NOT SO GOOD**
• Get your books before you start to read.	• Look for books when everyone else is reading.
• Choose books at your level.	• Choose books that are too hard.
• Pick a place where you are comfortable.	• Wander around the room.
• Stay in that place.	• Change places.
• Read "in your mind" or with a very low voice.	• Read in a loud voice.
• Save talking for later.	• Talk to people sitting near you.

Teacher Tip

See "Reading From Personal Book Box," page 25, for suggestions on how to help children choose books on their individual levels.

KF 1F 2F

Responding to Literature

Lesson Target

Young children need help understanding that reading is more than simply leafing through books. Reading involves not only attending to the text but also remembering parts of the story that have particular significance for the individual. Recording these responses and discussing them with others extends children's learning.

Why Teach This

Responding to literature and making connections is an important part of the complex process of learning to read.

Secondary Objective

- After children learn to record their responses, they can then learn about the give and take of discussing books.

Links to ELA Standards

- Students apply a wide range of strategies to comprehend, interpret, evaluate, and appreciate texts.
- Students read a wide range of print and nonprint texts to build an understanding of texts.
- Students employ a wide range of strategies as they write and use different writing process elements appropriately to communicate with different audiences.
- Students participate as knowledgeable, reflective, creative, critical members of a variety of literacy communities.

Learning Materials

- one piece of quality children's literature (for example, Eric Carle's *The Very Hungry Caterpillar*)
- paper
- crayons or markers

Time Range

15–25 minutes

Before You Start

Choose a book that children are already familiar with for this mini-lesson. Books that have young characters are also good choices. These include stories by Marc Brown, Mercer Mayer, or Nancy Carlson. Practice reading the book aloud before actually reading it to the class. It is always a good idea to run through a book before reading it to children.

Students' Prior Experience

Children have been introduced to routines for group read-alouds.

To Do

Gather children in the group meeting area and announce that you are going to read a story aloud.

Teacher Tip

It is a good idea to establish a routine for leaving the group meeting area, going to the writing center to get paper (and crayons or markers if these are not available at their tables), and walking to a table to work. Before introducing this routine to children, make sure that the traffic pattern from group to center to tables is clear and easy to follow.

TEACHING STRATEGIES

Drawing a response to literature is the first step of learning different ways to respond to a story. This is a typical response to literature for beginning kindergarten or first-grade students. As children develop the ability to write—even if they are only at the stage of writing one letter to represent one word—encourage them to add words to their drawings. After children have had several experiences responding to stories by drawing what they noticed, you can also ask them to draw

- the beginning of the story,
- the ending of the story,
- the main character,
- the problem of the story, or
- the solution to the story's problem.

Over time, responses to literature can be in written form. At this stage of children's writing, responses to literature can become more varied, responding to questions such as:

- *What would you do if you were _____?*
- *When did you first figure out that _____ was going to _____?*
- *What gave you that clue?*
- *What did you find funny (sad, scary, surprising, and so on) in the book?*

Show the front cover to the class and read the title and the author's name. Encourage the class to listen to the story very carefully because after they hear the story they are going to draw or write something about the story. Read the book aloud.

Say: *As I was reading this book, I noticed _____. If I were to draw a picture about this book, I would draw a picture of _____.* Ask the class: *What did you notice in the story as I was reading the book?*

Have students respond to the question, one at a time. After each child's comment, restate and expand on the comment. For example: *Jason noticed the fruit and the big, beautiful butterfly at the very end of the story. He might draw the butterfly really big in the middle of the page and put the fruit that the caterpillar ate around the sides.*

Ask children to draw the pictures they just described to the class. Dismiss a few children at a time to get paper and crayons or markers to create their response to that day's read-aloud.

Supporting Children's Learning

Virtually all kindergarten, first-, and second-grade students can choose one part of a book to draw or write about. For children who are having difficulties, sit with them one-on-one. Ask a child to look at the illustrations carefully and point to one illustration that she particularly liked. Turn the pages very slowly. When the child points to a particular illustration, ask her to tell you what she will draw. If she cannot remember from saying it aloud, let the child take the book to her table so she can glance at the illustration while she is drawing.

KF **1F** **2F**

Taking Turns Talking

Lesson Target
To help children understand that they must take turns talking during group meetings

Why Teach This
Young children find it hard to understand that they cannot say what they are thinking at the moment they think it. Adults have to help children learn that when they are in groups, sometimes it is appropriate to talk and sometimes it is not. Learning to take turns talking in groups is a skill that all children need to develop so that group learning times are effective.

Secondary Objective
• To help children learn ways of behaving respectfully toward each other

Link to ELA Standards
• Students participate as knowledgeable members of a variety of literacy communities.

Learning Materials
None

Time Range
10–15 minutes

Before You Start
Determine how you want children to take turns talking. You may have them raise their hand (or show a thumbs up, hold the class's "talking stick," display other physical action, and so on) when they want to say something in a group meeting. You may also want to coach children how to watch other people in the group and say something only when no one else is talking.

Students' Prior Experience
The class has discussed appropriate behavior for whole-group meetings, such as behaviors expected during read-alouds.

To Do
Gather children in the group meeting area and ask them to sit in a large circle. Ask all children to start talking when you give the thumbs-up signal and to stop talking when you give the thumbs-down signal. Repeat a few times. Ask: *Could you understand what was being said when everyone was talking at once? (No)*

Choose three children and ask them to start talking when you give the thumbs-up signal and to stop talking when you give the thumbs-down signal. Ask children if they could understand what was being said when the three people were talking at the same time. *(No)*

Ask: *How many people can you understand at any one time? (One)* Explain that for the class to understand what people are saying during meetings, children will need to take turns talking and to look and listen while someone else is talking. Say: *We are now going to practice taking turns talking. I'll ask one child at a time to talk while everyone else looks at and listens to him or her.*

Choose a simple sentence, such as: *Hi, my name is _____.* Ask all children to look at you and listen as you model saying the sentence. Announce that the child sitting to your left will go next. Look at that child and ask all the other children to look at him and listen also. Repeat until all children have had a turn.

Explain that the class will practice this for the next few days using a different sentence each day, e.g., *"My favorite dessert is _____," "I like to play _____," "My mother's name is _____,"* or *"I have _____ brothers and sisters."*

After doing this activity for two or three days, explain to the class that you are changing the way everyone takes a turn talking. Say: *Instead of talking if you are the next person in the circle, today I am going to ask you to raise your hand when you are ready to talk. When I nod at you, then it will be your turn to talk.*

Practice this several days in a row. At first, spend enough time so that every child who wants to say the sentence has the opportunity to do so. Gradually reduce the number of children who say the sentence so that children become accustomed to the idea that not everyone gets to talk during every group meeting.

Supporting Children's Learning

Learning to control oneself when wanting to say something terribly important is not easy for young children. This is a lesson that will have to be repeated many times. Still, even after most children appear to have learned self-control, some children need extra reminders.

Olivia was one such child. She had almost a compulsion to be the first to answer a question and she definitely wanted Mrs. Tarvin to call on her first. She repeatedly called out the answer or waved her hand in other children's faces or Mrs. Tarvin's face. Mrs. Tarvin and Olivia came to an agreement—Mrs. Tarvin would call on Olivia at least once during each class discussion if she could keep her self-control. They developed a "secret signal" between them (Mrs. Tarvin gestured to the floor with her palm down to indicate "settle down") and that seemed to help Olivia's impulsive behavior.

KW **1F** **2F**

Listening to Your Partner

Lesson Target
To teach behaviors expected of two people who are working together

Why Teach This
Giving children opportunities to listen for a purpose helps solidify their comprehension skills. Teaching young children to listen to another child read also helps them learn to follow the print across the page and collaborate with a peer while reinforcing their own learning.

Secondary Objective
• To show children that listening while a partner reads is an important comprehension strategy

Links to ELA Standards
• Students apply a wide range of strategies to comprehend texts.
• Students adjust their use of spoken language to communicate effectively with a variety of audiences and for different purposes.

Learning Materials
• books at children's appropriate reading levels (partners can have either two copies of the same book or two different books to read)
• chart tablet
• markers

Time Range

10–15 minutes

Before You Start

Work with two children so that they are prepared to role-play the listening activity in front of the whole class. Ask them to intentionally misread a couple of words that change the meaning of the text. Show them how to signal when they want the reader to stop and reread. For example, when the first child misreads a word, have the second child raise one finger and ask: *Could you please reread the last sentence?*

Students' Prior Experience

It is helpful for children to know about the give-and-take of working with a partner. Possible prior experiences include playing math games, co-creating murals, or co-building block structures.

Teacher Tip

As a whole-class activity, identify enough "private spaces" in the room so that children do not spend their reading time wandering around, searching for a place to sit. Mark these spaces with a self-adhesive note while the children "experiment" to see if it is a good private space. Make sure that the chosen spaces are not too close to each other and allow space for both children without being crowded. Once the spaces are identified, children know where to go without wasting instructional time.

To Do

Gather students in the group meeting area. Ask the two children to get ready to role-play listening to a partner read. Explain to the class that the first child will concentrate on reading the words while the second child listens to see if the story makes sense. Ask all children to do the job of the second child, listening to see if the story makes sense.

Have the two children begin. When the first child misreads a word, the second child raises one finger, as practiced earlier. She asks the first child to reread the last sentence, saying: *Could you please reread the last sentence?* Then, together they figure out the word that did not make sense and agree on how the word should be read.

Ask children to list the responsibilities of each partner, writing their responses on chart paper. The list might look something like the chart below:

Divide the class into partners. Ask each child to find an appropriate book to read, and then choose a private space so they can work as partners with one child practicing listening while the other one reads. Have

READER	LISTENER
Reader looks at the words.	Listener listens to the reader.
Reader uses strategies to figure out unknown words.	Listener checks to see if the story makes sense.
Reader keeps reading.	Listener stops the reader to question the meaning when necessary.

them switch roles so that each partner is both the reader and the listener.

Bring the class back to the meeting area to report how they did and to reread the list of responsibilities.

Supporting Children's Learning

Before a read-aloud, ask children to listen for miscues that you make as you read to the class. Obviously, you do not want this to become the focus of class read-alouds, but it is good to provide some extra practice for children in applying listening strategies to monitor for meaning and aid in comprehension.

KF **1F** **2F**

Getting Help

Lesson Target

To help children understand that there are several ways of getting questions answered or getting help that they need during the school day

Why Teach This

Many young children think that the teacher is the only person who can answer their questions or help them in any way. These children are at a distinct disadvantage. They must wait until you have a spare moment and then must catch your attention before another child does. When you equip children with many strategies for getting help, most children get their questions answered more quickly and return to the reading assignments they are working on.

Secondary Objective

• To reduce interruptions as you work with individuals or small groups of children

Link to ELA Standards

• Students participate as knowledgeable members of a variety of literacy communities.

Learning Materials

• chart tablet
• markers

Time Range

15–20 minutes

Before You Start

Think about possible strategies children might use for requesting help from another student during reading time. (See "To Do" below for some ideas.) Jot them down for reference when leading the class in this discussion.

Students' Prior Experience

Children have been introduced to routines for group meetings and taking turns talking.

To Do

Gather children in the group meeting area. Mention that you noticed how some children have to wait a long time for your attention when they need help. Ask them to think of other ways they could get answers to their questions or obtain other types of help. Write children's suggestions on chart paper. Guide children into suggesting such strategies as:

• Ask someone at your table.
• Ask an expert in the class.

Teacher Tip

Designate one or two children in the class as the "expert" on different issues. For example, your class might have an expert at sharpening pencils, an expert at getting more paper for the writing center, an expert at changing the date on the date stamp, an expert at refilling the stapler, an expert at finding books, and so on.

- Try the reading strategies we have learned (refer to posted charts).
- Mark the word you can't read with a self-adhesive note and keep reading.

Help children identify times when they can ask you their questions. Possible times include when their reading group is working with you, during their individual reading conference, and so on. List these on chart paper, too.

Together reread all of the strategies, then suggest that children practice using these strategies for getting help in the next few days. Hold another meeting later to add more strategies children think of and delete strategies that do not seem to work. Post the chart in the room for future reference.

Supporting Children's Learning

When a child forgets what to do when he needs help, ask that child to meet you at the "Getting Help" chart and read the suggestions together. Ask the child to focus on one reading strategy that might work and try that one. Or refer the child to another who can remind him of some possible reading strategies to consider.

Of course, reading time is not the only time during the day when children need help. Use variations of these activities for other subject areas are well. The more independent children become, the more learning they will discover on their own.

KS **1W** **2F**

Reading From Personal Book Box

Lesson Target
To have each child spend time daily reading books at his or her individual reading level

Why Teach This
In a way, reading is much like learning anything else. If a child is learning to play the piano, she most likely takes lessons, practices certain skills every day, and actually plays the piano. Children who are learning to read need instruction, need to practice new skills, and need to actually read books at their level. Reading from personal book boxes provides this time for children to actually read.

Secondary Objective
- To help children learn to choose books at their own reading level

Link to ELA Standards
- Students read a wide range of print and nonprint texts to build an understanding of texts.

Teacher Tip
The difference between DEAR time and "Reading From Personal Book Box" is the type of books that children are allowed to read during those times. During DEAR time, children can read anything in the classroom, including books for grown-ups (they can learn information from quality photographs), magazines, class-created books, and so on. During "Reading From Personal Book Box" time, only books that children can read independently should be in their book boxes and only these books should be read. Guide children's selection of books through book talks and direct instruction.

Learning Materials

- plastic or cardboard magazine holder for each student
- large selection of books at different reading levels
- colored dot stickers
- permanent markers
- self-adhesive notes

Time Range

15–20 minutes

Before You Start

Gather sufficient numbers of books at all reading levels appropriate for your class. Sort the books into large plastic tubs that are labeled by reading level. Mark each book with its reading level using permanent markers on color-coded dot stickers. If individual books are not identified, children will have difficulty putting them back in the correct containers.

Before this lesson, choose one book for each child at the correct reading level. Put a self-adhesive note with a child's name on each book so you can quickly distribute books.

Decide where to store the personal book boxes in the classroom.

To Do

Gather children in the group meeting area. Show children the new containers that will be used as book boxes. Introduce the lesson by saying something like: *Everyone in this class will get his or her own personal book box. The only things that will go in your box are books that are at your reading level; in other words, books that you can read all by yourself.*

Explain to children that you will meet with small groups during reading-choice time to help them choose five or six books that are exactly at their level. But for the moment, you will give each child his or her own book box and one book at the correct reading level. Distribute the book boxes, then give each child the book you selected.

Ask children to look around the classroom for a place that seems special to them—a place where they can be a serious reader. Say: *In just a minute, I will ask you to find that special place. Please keep in mind that this has to be a*

Teacher Tip

Few classrooms have sufficient space in one place to store boxes for every child in the class. Consider storing the book boxes in five or six different places in the room. This eliminates "traffic jams" when children are asked to get or to put away their book boxes.

Teacher Tip

It is easy to teach young readers how to choose just-right books if children have access to a leveled library where every book is labeled. If organized, leveled books are not available, you might teach children to use the five-finger rule: Begin reading a page of a potential book. When you reach a word you can't read, hold up one finger. Continue reading and holding up another finger for each word you cannot read on that page. If you are holding up five fingers and you are still reading the same page, then you need to look for another book.

personal spot. You cannot sit next to another person. Dismiss children to find their special place. Be prepared to help children who choose the same place negotiate a compromise.

After children are settled, tell them to practice reading to themselves for three minutes. Set a kitchen timer and tell the class that you do not expect to hear anything during that time. When the timer rings, show children where to store their boxes, then dismiss them a few at a time to put their book boxes away.

Supporting Children's Learning

Some children may have difficulty sitting still and attending to only the books in their boxes. One strategy is to choose a place to sit in the classroom where there are fewer distractions. You may need to set different times for different children.

Teacher Tip

Unless you have more than 100 Level A books (according to the Fountas and Pinnell leveling system), you may want to wait to offer this reading choice until some children can read Level B and C books.

 What Experts Say About...

Independent Reading

- For children to stay engaged in reading for many minutes, they need books that are at their "just right" reading level and that interest them. To create collections of leveled books refer to Fountas and Pinnell's *Matching Books to Readers (Heinemann, 1999).*

- Struggling readers have usually not been provided multiple books at their reading level and time in class to read and reread these books.

- Children should be able to read a book with 90 percent accuracy for that book to be considered at their independent reading level.

- Students need time every day to read books at their independent reading level.

Sources: Allington, 2001; Taberski, 2000

Establishing Routines for the Year

KF **1F**

Taking Attendance

Lesson Target
To help children learn to recognize their names in print

Why Teach This
Children first learn how to read the words that are most important to them. The one word that means the most to a young child is his or her own name. Learning to read one's own name—and the names of classmates—begins the process of helping children see themselves as readers.

Secondary Objectives
- To help children learn to recognize their classmates' names in print
- To introduce and reinforce initial letter sounds in names
- To support children as they learn the concept of words and begin attending to the number of letters in words

Link to ELA Standards
- Students read a wide range of print and nonprint texts to build an understanding of texts.

Learning Materials
- sentence strips
- pocket chart
- markers
- gallon-size reclosable plastic bag

Time Range
10–15 minutes

Absent	At School

Before You Start
Carefully print children's first and last names on sentence strips. Cut the names apart. Prepare sentence strips that say "Absent" and "At School." Store all of these in a reclosable plastic bag and place near the group meeting area. Move a pocket chart near the group meeting area so that all children can see the names in the chart.

Students' Prior Experience
Children have been introduced to routines for group meetings.

To Do

Gather children in the group meeting area. Tell children that every classroom in the school has to turn in a report to the office that tells the principal who is at school and who is absent.

Show children the plastic bag with all the name cards. Explain that there is one name card for every child in the class. Every morning the class will meet in the group meeting area to determine who is absent and to fill out that report form.

Pick a name card from the bag one at a time and show it to the class, asking children to watch for their name and to say their name aloud when they see it. Prompt children who need additional support to recognize their name. After a child "reads" his name, place the name card in the pocket chart under the label "At School."

After all children who are present have read their names, place the cards of children who are absent in the pocket chart under the label "Absent." Model copying the names of the children who are absent on the attendance form and ask two children to take the form to the school office.

Expanding the Lesson

As soon as any child in the class is capable of copying names, enlist her to start filling out the attendance form to submit to the office. Young children need to be involved in writing for multiple purposes as soon as possible.

Supporting Children's Learning

It may take some time for children to learn to recognize their names. Some children in the class may learn to read all the student names before other children consistently recognize their own name. Give extra support to children who are having difficulty reading their own name, suggesting what they should look for. For example, you might say: *Samantha, you have a long name that starts with an* S. *Watch all the name cards for a name that starts with that* S *shape.*

KF **1F** **2F**

Reading the Morning Message

Lesson Target
To teach children how to attend to text

Why Teach This
As young children watch adults write, they learn that adults always start writing at the top of the page, writing left to right with a return sweep. They also learn that writing is "talk written down." Young children typically have more interest in trying to read text that relates directly to them. When teachers write interesting messages, children look forward to trying to figure out what each morning message says.

Secondary Objectives
- To focus children's attention on concepts of print or forms of print
- To increase children's sight-word vocabularies

Links to ELA Standards

- Students read a wide range of print to acquire new information.
- Students apply a wide range of strategies to comprehend text. They draw on prior experience, their interactions with other readers and writers, their knowledge of word meaning and of other texts, their word identification strategies, and their understanding of textual features.

Learning Materials

- chart tablet, white board, or chalkboard
- felt-tip markers, dry-erase markers, or chalk

Time Range

5–10 minutes

Before You Start

Decide what the morning message will be and plan questions to ask children.

Students' Prior Experience

Children know the concepts related to the questions you will ask.

To Do

Gather children in the group meeting area and direct their attention to you as you write. Write the morning message, saying each word as you write it. Occasionally, make side comments about sounds associated with letters, punctuation, word choice, and so on. Reread the morning message. Ask questions such as:

- *How many sentences did I write today?*
- *How can you tell how many sentences there are?*
- *What is this mark I made at the end of this sentence?*
- *Are there any words that begin with the same letter?*
- *Which word is longest?*

Vary the questions you ask from day to day.

Teacher Tip

Try these suggestions for making morning message more interesting for children:

- Use children's names in the messages.
- Relate the new message to previous class activities.
- Use a variety of questions and statements.
- Announce class activities through morning message.
- Search for odd or interesting facts that appeal to children.

Expanding the Lesson

When you first introduce morning messages, write simple sentences. Then as children's skills increase, write increasingly complex sentences that allow children to apply recently learned knowledge and skills.

Supporting Children's Learning

If children have difficulty answering these types of questions, spend a few minutes with just those children—after dismissing the others from the group—rereading the morning message and showing children how to find the answer to each question asked that day.

KF 1F 2F

Taking Books Home

Lesson Target
To emphasize to children the importance of reading at home every night

Why Teach This
Supporting children's reading at home reinforces the idea that reading is not just a school activity. When children read at home, they are learning the lifelong habit of reading for a variety of reasons—pleasure, information, relaxation, and so on. Encourage each child's family to spend a few minutes every evening reading with their child. The support of a child's family in his or her development as a reader is important.

Secondary Objectives
- To increase reading fluency and comprehension
- To help children develop a sense of responsibility for learning materials and for their own learning

Link to ELA Standards
- Students read a wide range of print and nonprint texts to build an understanding of texts.

Learning Materials
- collection of books suitable for children to take home to read *
- gallon-size reclosable plastic bags
- Book Log (page 35)
- chart tablet
- markers

* These might be texts provided by the basal reading series or leveled books from other sources. Your school library is a good resource for extra titles. Book clubs also sell inexpensive books leveled by children's abilities.

Time Range
10–15 minutes

Before You Start
Decide what procedures you want to implement for checking out books to take home. Consider where in the classroom to store the books, how children will select a "just right" book, how you will monitor the books they read, and where children will put the book after they select it. Prepare several books

Teacher Tip
See page 33 for a sample letter to send to families, stressing the importance of their role in supporting their child's development as a reader. Also, page 34 contains a sample family letter about setting up a routine for using take-home books.

Teacher Tip
Creating guidelines for taking books home is a good opportunity to introduce contracts to students. Type the guidelines using children's exact language. Add three lines at the bottom of the contract for your signature, the child's signature, and a parent's signature.

(at least three times the number of children in the class) by putting each one in a separate reclosable plastic bag. Put bags in a container labeled "Take-Home Books," and put the container in a place that is easily accessible for all children. Provide copies of the Book Log form for all children.

Students' Prior Experience
You and your students should have a conversation about taking care of books.

 What Experts Say About...

Reading Comprehension

- Children need explicit instruction on comprehension strategies such as summarizing the main idea, predicting outcomes in text, drawing inferences, and self-monitoring for misunderstandings.
- Comprehension instruction can occur when adults read to children as well as when children read themselves.
- Common comprehension strategies—such as stopping to think about what you're reading, story mapping, and using writing to help understand what you're reading—should be modeled for children during read alouds.
- When a child retells a story, this gives teachers a good idea of a child's ability to comprehend that story.
- Teachers should provide young children significant support initially, then move them closer and closer to independence.
- Children need to have words in their oral vocabularies if they are to comprehend those words in continuous texts.
- Comprehension can break down at the word level or text level. If accuracy is below 95 percent, the problem is most likely at the word level—the child is focused on decoding the words that he does not attend to their meaning. If the accuracy is above 95 percent, it may be that the text level is beyond the child's comprehension.

Sources: Allington, 2001; Burns, Griffin, & Snow, 1999; Taberski, 2000

To Do
Gather children in the group meeting area. Begin the discussion by saying: *You are reading a lot of books at school, and some of you wondered about sharing those books with your family. So starting next Monday, each of you will be taking a book to read at home.*

Discuss guidelines for taking books home. Ask children for suggestions and record their comments on chart paper. Some suggestions children might make (or you might mention) include:
- Take one book at a time.
- Ask your family to listen to you only when they are not busy.
- Find a quiet place to read that is not next to the TV.
- Read the book aloud to someone who lives with you.
- Write down the title of the book when you finish.
- Bring the book back the next day.
- If you lose a book, you have to replace it.
Reread the guidelines to the class and vote to select the ones the class wants to use. Model how a child would select a book, read it, and record the title and other information on the Book Log sheet. Also model how to include the plastic bag with other items to take home (in backpacks, in cubby, in locker, and so on).

Supporting Children's Learning
When children forget the routine for selecting a take-home book, refer them to other children who have internalized the routine.

A letter from your child's teacher

Why Reading at Home Is Important

Dear Families:

The number of minutes a child spends reading at home every night doesn't seem like it would make a major difference in his or her learning. But let's compare two students, and look at the issue mathematically:

Student 1 reads 20 minutes a night, five nights a week.
Student 2 reads only 4 minutes a night, five nights a week…or not at all.

Step 1: Multiply minutes a night by 5 times each week.
Student 1 reads 20 minutes x 5 times a week = 100 minutes/week
Student 2 reads 4 minutes x 5 times a week = 20 minutes/week

Step 2: Multiply minutes a week by 4 weeks each month.
Student 1 reads 400 minutes a month.
Student 2 reads 80 minutes a month.

Step 3: Multiply minutes a month by 9 months in a school year.
Student 1 reads 3,600 minutes in a school year.
Student 2 reads 720 minutes in a school year.

Student 1 practices reading the equivalent of 10 whole school days a year.
Student 2 gets the equivalent of only two school days of reading practice.

By the end of sixth grade, if Student 1 and Student 2 maintain these same reading habits—not counting reading on the weekends or during summer vacations:
Student 1 will have read the equivalent of 60 whole school days.
Student 2 will have read the equivalent of only 12 school days.

One would expect the gap of information retained to have widened considerably and undoubtedly school performance, too. Some questions to ponder:
Which student would you expect to read better?
Which student would you expect to know more?
Which student would you expect to write better?
Which student would you expect to have a better vocabulary?
Which student would you expect to be more successful in school…and in life?

I hope that this will help you insist that your child read for at least 20 minutes at home every night.

Sincerely,

Take-Home Books

Dear Families:

Starting next Monday, your child will be bringing home a different book every night. It will be in a plastic bag to help protect it. These are special books that I call our "Take-Home Books." From the "Take-Home Book" basket, children will choose the book that they want to take home to read to their families. These are books the children have practiced reading in class so your child should be able to read it aloud to you.

You may think that the books your child brings home are too easy for him or her and that your child should be working on reading more challenging books. We don't need to worry about that at this point. We want children to feel comfortable reading to other people. We also do not need to worry if a child chooses the same book over and over again. I will address these two issues after children have been taking home books for several weeks.

There will be a Book Log in each child's folder. The children have all agreed to keep a list of the "Take-Home Books" that they read every night. Your child should write the date and copy the title of the book onto the Book Log, and you should sign your initials beside the title so we can remember who listened to each child read. A home routine that usually works well is asking your child to read to you first, then you read a book to him or her.

Thank you for making this new routine a part of your family's life. This is just one more step in helping your child become a competent, confident lifelong learner.

Sincerely,

_____'s Book Log

Date	Title of Book	Initials

CHAPTER TWO

For Emergent Readers

Overview

Many experts believe that children are learning to read from the time they are infants. As adults read to infants and toddlers, young children begin to develop important concepts about reading. As preschoolers converse with adults, learn nursery rhymes and songs, and continue to listen to read-alouds, they learn even more about literacy. When children enter school, they are introduced to more systematic reading instruction. They are taught specific lessons about reading concepts and skills. Throughout the period from infancy until the time children are actually reading small books, they are considered emergent readers.

Activities and routines for emergent readers focus more on beginning reading strategies than the beginning-of-the-year routines did. At this stage, children are ready to concentrate on skills, learning ways to make the text more accessible.

Checklist of Signs of Late-Stage Emergent Readers

❑ **1.** Child has some reading behaviors such as turning pages from front to back.

❑ **2.** Child pretends to read.

❑ **3.** Child draws and/or writes at an early writing stage (scribbling, pretend letters, random letters), then "reads" what he or she has written.

❑ **4.** Child identifies text as what is read on the page.

❑ **5.** Child knows that text is read left to right and top to bottom.

❑ **6.** Child can point to one word, the first word in a sentence, one letter, and the first letter in a word.

❑ **7.** Child can recognize some words, e.g., own name, names of other children in the class, words that are important to him or her.

❑ **8.** Child hears rhyme and can make up a rhyming word for a word given.

❑ **9.** Child can name many letters and can give a word that begins with some common sounds.

* Checklist adapted from Cunningham & Allington, 1994

Strategies for Emergent Readers

KF **1F**

Saying "What I Noticed"

Lesson Target
To encourage children to examine the illustrations of a children's book and make comments about their observations

Why Teach This
Using illustrations as a clue for determining an unknown word is one of the first reading strategies young children learn. Teaching children to observe illustrations for details, comment on the details they see, and listen to peers' observations all serve as important foundations for beginning readers.

Secondary Objective
• To help children learn to use illustrations as support for the text, specifically as clues for decoding unknown words

Link to ELA Standards
• Students participate as knowledgeable, reflective, creative, critical members of a variety of literacy communities.

Learning Material
• any high-quality children's book with strong illustrations

Time Range
15–20 minutes

Before You Start
Carefully select a children's book with strong illustrations that support the story line. For example, *A Snowy Day* by Ezra Jack Keats (Viking, 1996), *Owl Moon* by Jane Yolen (Philomel, 1987), or *The Relatives Came* by Cynthia Rylant (Simon & Schuster, 1993).

Students' Prior Experience
Children have been introduced to routines for group meetings and taking turns talking in the group.

To Do
Gather children in the group meeting area. Explain that you will be looking at a picture book and noticing the pictures or illustrations in it. Display the front cover of the book and describe the illustrations. Ask children to predict what the story might be about based on the pictures (or painting, drawing, or photograph) on the front cover.

◄ **Expanding the Lesson** ►

After children have had several opportunities to say what they notice about an illustration and discuss illustrations/stories, ask them to record what they notice by drawing or writing.

Starting with the first page of the story, do a picture walk-through of the book. Tell the story and point to the part of each illustration that supports your comments. In this way, you model the types of comments appropriate for children to make when they review a particular illustration.

Return to the first page of the story and ask: *Do you think that everyone notices the same thing when they look at this picture?* Ask one child what she notices about this first illustration. Point to the particular part of the illustration the child comments about. Ask two or three other children the same question, pointing to parts of the illustration they notice.

Turn to the next page and continue asking several children to say what they notice when they look at this particular illustration. Suggest that children apply this technique of "noticing" when they are reading independently.

Supporting Children's Learning

Children with limited literacy experiences need more adult modeling of the process of looking at illustrations and commenting on them. Support them by giving simple directions such as: *Find the _____. Point to the _____.* Work with small groups so each child can examine illustrations more closely and interact more often.

KS **1W** **2F**

Thinking in Your Brain

Lesson Target

To help children stop and think about answers to questions before immediately saying the first thing they think of

Why Teach This

In whole-group situations, a few higher-ability children typically dominate the group as they answer questions posed by the teacher. These children tend to think faster than other children and are often impulsive, answering before they even think about the question. All children need opportunities to answer your questions. The technique of "thinking in your brain" gives all children in the class extra time to mull over answers to teacher-posed questions before responding.

Secondary Objective

• To think more deeply and more reflectively about answers to questions

Link to ELA Standards

• Students participate as knowledgeable, reflective, creative, critical members of a variety of literacy communities.

Learning Material

• one book that is familiar to most, if not all, students

Time Range

5–10 minutes

Before You Start

Plan a few open-ended questions to pose during this lesson. Develop them so children will have to reflect on their thoughts before immediately answering. Suggested questions include:

- *Who is the most interesting character in the book and why?*
- *How did the characters feel about each other and how do you know that?*
- *Are the characters believable? Why or why not?*
- *How is the main character like other characters you've read about?*
- *How is the setting of this book like another place you know?*
- *How important is the setting to this book and why?*
- *How is this book like another book you've read?*
- *How did the author engage the reader at the beginning of the story?*
- *What is the high point of the story and why?*
- *What lesson does this book teach about life?*
- *Why do you think the author wrote this book?*
- *How would the story be different if it was written from another character's perspective?*
- *What is another possible ending for the story?*

Students' Prior Experience

Children have had many opportunities to hear stories and answer different types of questions about those stories.

To Do

Gather children in the group meeting area. Explain that the class is going to try a new way of answering questions—they are going to think a long time before answering any of the questions.

Tell children that you will ask a question and you will count to ten while they "think in their brain." When the time is up, you will give the signal of pointing at the group of children. At that time, they can raise their hand (or show a thumb or use some other signal) if they want to answer the question.

Ask three or four questions similar to the ones under "Before You Start." Repeat this activity with the class every day for a week or two.

Supporting Children's Learning

Use the term "think in your brain" at other times during the day. For example, during a math lesson suggest that a child "think in his brain" while he is computing the answer. Extend this idea of "thinking in your brain" to silent reading. Ask children to "read in their brain" so that no one else in the class can hear what they are reading. As children become more familiar with the phrase, they will apply it to more situations.

Teacher Tip

In most elementary-school classes, the delay between the time a teacher asks a question and the first answer from a student is about one or two seconds. This does not give many children enough time to process the question and consider what they think an answer might be. Increasing the wait time to five seconds dramatically affects some children's ability to answer questions. Initially, try to give ten seconds between question and first answer to emphasize the idea of "thinking in your brain."

Whole- and Small-Group Reading Activities

(KW) (1F) (2F)

Using the Word Wall

Lesson Target

To provide a resource for children to read and spell high-frequency words

Why Teach This

Beginning readers are often intimidated when they see a page of text with a lot of words on the page. However, when their sight-word vocabulary is moderate to large, they already know how to read many of the words on the page. Working with word-wall words helps children understand patterns and relationships among words, thus building their sight-word vocabularies.

Secondary Objectives

• To increase sight-word vocabularies
• To use as a resource for word study

Link to ELA Standards

• Students apply knowledge of language structure and language conventions to discuss print texts.

Learning Materials

• word wall
• four or five sight words (difficulty of words depends on the grade level, e.g., for

Teacher Tip

If wall space is scarce, consider using three-panel display boards. If attaching words on the word wall with Velcro® strips is a problem, try putting library-card pockets under word-wall words and placing copies of the word in the pocket. This way, children can take a correctly spelled word from the word wall to their tables as they are writing, then return it when they are finished.

introducing the word wall to kindergarten students, use *I*, *a*, *an*, and *the*; for first-grade students, use *at*, *in*, *can*, and *and*; and for second-grade students, use *that*, *what*, *here*, and *they*)

Time Range

15–20 minutes

Before You Start

Create a word wall, keeping in mind some of the following guidelines:

- Have a distinct space for each letter of the alphabet.
- Mark the spaces with both the upper- and lowercase letter.
- Some spaces will need to be larger than others. For example, the *W* space needs to be larger than the *Q* space.
- Spaces need to be posted low enough so that all children can reach all words on the word wall.

Students' Prior Experience

Children have been introduced to routines for group meetings and, for the most part, understand the process of taking turns talking.

To Do

Gather children in front of the word wall. Ask: *What do you notice about the new bulletin board (or display board)?* Children might comment that it has all the letters in the alphabet, it has both capital and lowercase letters, each letter is in a different box, and so on. Tell children that this special place, called the "word wall," is where the class will keep words that they know how to read.

Tell children that every Monday they will get four or five new words and that every day they will play a game using the words on the word wall.

Expanding the Lesson

To support children's ability to remember words from the word wall, begin with words from favorite rhymes, poems, chants, songs, or stories. To encourage children to use the word wall in their reading and writing activities, model ways to use it.

 What Experts Say About...

Word Walls

- Word walls are cumulative, as new words are added weekly.
- Word walls have different purposes: word analysis, models of correctly spelled words, and vocabulary building.
- Word walls have great potential for transferring the responsibility of learning to read words from the teacher to students.
- Word-wall activities should be fast-paced and last only a few minutes.
- Activities that incorporate word-wall words provide scaffolding that structures the ways that children think about and use words.
- Because children work with word-wall words repeatedly, these words go into children's long-term memories.

Sources: Brabham & Villaume, 2001; Cunningham, Hall, & Sigmon, 1999; Pinnell & Fountas, 1998; Stahl, 1992; Wagstaff, 1998

Word-Wall Activities

- Have children create portable, personal word walls by opening a file folder and dividing each of the four sides into six sections, putting *X*, *Y*, and *Z* in the same section. As you post a new word on the class wall, instruct children to write it in the corresponding section of their personal word wall. When you conduct an individual writing conference, suggest that the child add the words you discussed to her personal word wall. Encourage children to add to their personal word walls as any spelling discussions occur. This way, children can take the word wall with them wherever they are writing: outside, in the library, or at home.

- Have children read the word, spell it (clapping one clap per letter, or snapping their fingers, stomping their feet, and so on), and read the word again.

- Play "Guess My Word." Have children write numerals 1 through 5 down the left side of a piece of paper. Give children clues for the word that you are thinking about (it must be on the word wall), making the answer more and more obvious with each successive clue. Have children write down their guess after hearing each clue. For example, for the word *they*, you might say:

  1. *It is a word on the word wall.*
  2. *It has one syllable.*
  3. *It starts with a digraph.*
  4. *It ends with the long-a sound, but it is not spelled with an* A.
  5. *It means more than one person.*

- Have children point to a word, say it, clap the syllables, then repeat the word.

- If children are having difficulty clapping syllables, ask them to put their fingers under their chin and count the number of times their jaw drops as they say the word. This method is a bit more concrete for kinesthetic learners.

- When introducing the concept of syllables, use two or three two-syllable words from the word wall. Write the words on sentence strips. Read one word to the class, then cut it into syllables. Put the word in a slot in a pocket chart with a piece of different-colored sentence strip between the two parts of the word. Have the class read the word together. Repeat with other words.

- When the word wall has several words under each letter, teach small groups of children to play "Last Letter First." In this activity, the first child reads a word from the word wall. The next child takes the last letter of that word, then finds and reads a word from the word wall that begins with that letter. Continue until each child in the group has had at least one turn.

- Post a simple picture or drawing next to the nouns or verbs that lend themselves to this. For example, beside *boy* draw a stick figure of a boy; next to the word *run* sketch a person with knees and arms bent in a running pose.

Continue to explain that soon every single child in the class will be reading the word-wall words.

Explain that each word has to be put in the correct box on the word wall. If the word starts with an *A*, that word has to be placed in the *Aa* box; if the word starts with a *B*, that word has to be placed in the *Bb* box; and so on.

Show the class one of the word-wall words (choose the simplest word to build children's confidence in their reading) and ask children to read this word together. Give the word to a child and ask her to place the word in the correct box on the word wall. Repeat with all of that week's words for the word wall.

On successive days, teach children how to play the word-wall activities listed in the Teaching Strategies box on page 42.

Supporting Children's Learning

Be patient with children who do not remember the word-wall routines. Simply repeat the routine until all children remember it.

Expanding the Lesson

To reinforce children's ability to add word-wall words to their sight vocabularies, create Concentration-type games using several of the words. Make two copies of six words from the word wall on cards. Have children shuffle the cards, placing them on the table or floor in three rows of four cards. The first player turns over two cards and reads them. If the cards match, that player keeps the cards and gets another turn. If not, that player turns those cards back over—in the same places—and the second player gets a turn. Play continues until all word pairs have been taken by the players.

KS **1F**

Being the Words

Lesson Target

To recognize high-frequency words

Why Teach This

Establishing the basic procedure of participating in "Being the Words" enables children to quickly complete the activity. "Being the Words" helps students recognize often-used words and learn word order.

Secondary Objectives

- To increase phonological awareness
- To learn the conventions of punctuation
- To learn the conventions of capitalization

Link to ELA Standards

- Students draw on their understanding of textual features (e.g. sound–letter correspondence, sentence structure, context, graphics).

Learning Materials

- index cards
- markers
- a familiar book (such as *Brown Bear, Brown Bear, What Do You See?* by Bill Martin, Jr.)

Time Range

10–15 minutes

Before You Start

Write all the words from the book selection on index cards, one word per card. Make duplicate cards for words used more than once or with changes in capitalization. Make separate cards for the punctuation marks that are needed.

Students' Prior Experience

Children should have heard the text enough times that they can chorally read the portion of the text selected for this activity.

To Do

Gather children in the group meeting area and distribute the word cards to them. Explain that some cards have words, some have punctuation marks, and that both are necessary to make a sentence.

Open the book to the page containing the familiar text. For example, in *Brown Bear, Brown Bear, What Do You See?* turn to the page that actually says, "Brown Bear, Brown Bear, What do you see?"

Tell children that they are going to "be the words" and will make this sentence for the class to read. Indicate an area at the front of the group meeting area for children to stand. (The edge of the rug that defines the group area is a good place.)

Ask children to read aloud the familiar text from the book as you point to the words. (You may also want to write the sentence on chart paper so all children can see the words better.) Have children look at their cards to see if their word matches any of the words in the text. Encourage those children to move to the area in front and to arrange themselves in left-to-right order, re-creating the sentence. When everyone is in the correct order, ask children who are not standing to read the sentence as you move behind each child who is "being a word."

Depending on children's ability, give the same words to different children so they can re-create the sentence or continue with subsequent sentences from the text. Explain that the same words are used over and over in sentences. Tell children that when they pay very close attention to words in "Being the Words" they will learn to read many different words.

Supporting Children's Learning

Some children may have trouble finding their "spot" within the sentence. Mark numbered spaces on the floor, then have the child count words in the sentence until he reaches his word. Have him repeat that number, then go and stand on that number on the floor. For example, if a child had the word *What* in the sentence, "Brown Bear, Brown Bear, What do you see?" support him as he counts the words up to *What* (number 5), then stands on the numeral 5 on the floor.

(KS) (1F) (2F)

Making Words

Lesson Target

To use knowledge of letter sounds and follow oral directions to manipulate letters/phonemes to create words

Why Teach This

Hundreds of words can be spelled based on the knowledge of a few words and understanding word patterns. This activity provides frequent manipulation of letters and words, helping children recognize common English word patterns.

Secondary Objectives

- To help children learn to spell simple words (often used to begin this activity) correctly
- To increase children's sight-word vocabularies

Link to ELA Standards

- Students draw on their understanding of textual features (e.g. sound–letter correspondence, sentence structure, context, graphics).

Learning Materials

- pocket chart
- letters of the "Secret Word of the Day" written on index cards
- chart tablet or white board
- sets of the letters of the "Secret Word of the Day" for each child

Time Range

15–20 minutes

Before You Start

For each "Making Words" lesson, decide on the final "secret" word to use for the day—perhaps a word that ties to the curriculum or a word that represents a particular interest of children in the class, such as *caterpillar*, *neighborhood*, or *airplane*. List other words that can be made from the letters in the secret word, looking for little words, words that represent a pattern, and longer words. Group them by length, keeping together words with two letters, three letters, four letters, and so on. Plan a sequence for introducing 10 to 15 words so that words can be created by changing or adding one letter from one word to the next.

Students' Prior Experience

Children need experience in listening to oral directions and following them relatively quickly.

To Do

Have children sit at their desk or table, cleared of other materials. Tell children that they will be making words using the letters that you give them. Distribute the day's letters to each child. Review the vowels each child has, then review the consonants. For this first lesson, the secret word will be *caterpillar*, so the letters each child should have are: *a, a, e, i, c, l, l, p, r, r, t.* Put these letters (written on index cards) in the top pocket of the pocket chart.

Ask children to line up their letters, then pull down the two letters that make the word *it*. Ask one child to demonstrate pulling down those same letters in the pocket chart into the second row of pockets on the pocket chart. At the same time, have another child write *it* on chart paper.

Continue asking children who are working at their desks to change one letter to create the following words: *it, at, cat, pat, rat, rate, rare, race, pace,* and *place*. For each word, have one child create the new word in the pocket chart and another write it on the chart paper. As a final challenge, tell children that all the letters combined make the "Secret Word of the Day." Give clues to help them arrange the letters to form the secret word, such as: */C-c-c/ begins the word*, or *the first syllable is /cat/*. If this is too challenging for children, simply tell them the secret word and spell it for them as they rearrange the letters to form that word.

Supporting Children's Learning

Some children will have difficulty keeping up with the pace of this activity from oral directions alone. Have these children sit close to the pocket chart so the movement of the letters as words are created in the chart serves as a model.

Reading Songs

Lesson Target

To support children's belief that they are readers by conducting choral readings of familiar songs

Why Teach This

Many young children need their teacher's support to learn to accept themselves as readers. Choral reading of familiar songs helps children see themselves as readers. They can memorize words to a song rather quickly, so they can then participate in the choral reading of song lyrics. Whether they could read these particular words out of the context of the song is not the point.

They can "read" the words in this context, boosting their confidence as readers.

Secondary Objective

• To learn high-frequency words

Link to ELA Standards

• Students read a wide range of print and nonprint texts to build an understanding of texts.

Learning Materials

• books with texts that are the lyrics of familiar songs
• chart tablet
• markers

Time Range

10–15 minutes

Before You Start

Gather two or three books that use familiar song lyrics as their text. For example:
• *Baby Beluga* by Raffi (Crown, 1997)
• *Down by the Bay* by Raffi (Crown, 1999)
• *The Wheels on the Bus* by Paul O. Zelinsky (Dutton, 1990)
• *If You're Happy and You Know It, Clap Your Hands!* by David Carter (Cartwheel, 1997)
• *This Land Is Your Land* by Woody Guthrie (Little Brown, 1998)

Print each song's lyrics on separate sheets of chart paper and laminate for durability. Select one to introduce in the first "Reading Songs" lesson.

> ### Teacher Tip
> See page 49 for a sample letter to send to families stressing the importance of children believing they are readers.

Twinkle, Twinkle, Little Star

Twinkle, twinkle, little star,

How I wonder what you are,

Up above the world so high,

Like a diamond in the sky.

Twinkle, twinkle, little star,

How I wonder what you are.

Convincing Children They Are Readers

Dear Families:

Does your child view himself or herself as a reader? Is your child confident in his or her ability to read? Since most children this age do not view themselves as readers, I am doing several things in the classroom to encourage children to think of themselves as readers. You can support your child's learning by doing some of these things at home as well.

I point out times when the children use reading. They know where the cafeteria is because the sign on the door says "cafeteria." The same is true for the computer lab, nurse's office, and so on.

When I am reading a familiar story, I encourage children to join with me, reading the parts they have memorized. I don't say, "Just say the parts you've memorized." Rather, I just indicate with a hand gesture that they should read with me.

You can encourage your child to read parts of familiar books. Saying "Wow! I didn't know you were reader! Look how you read the words on that page," establishes the idea in your child's mind that he or she is capable of reading.

Sincerely,

Students' Prior Experience

Children have been introduced to routines for group meetings. Children have sung (or listened to) the songs enough times that they have the lyrics memorized.

Teacher Tip

Copy or type (in a large font) the lyrics of the familiar songs being used with the class. Add personal sketches or clip art (or get one or two children to draw an illustration) to identify the song without necessarily having to read the title conventionally.

Make a copy of "Twinkle, Twinkle, Little Star" (page 48) and put a copy in the class's poetry binder and/or in the listening center (along with an audiotape of the class's choral reading of that song). Also send home copies of the lyrics so children can start a poetry binder of their own at home.

To Do

Gather children in the group meeting area. Explain that you are going to read a book to them and they need to listen very carefully because you think they can join you in reading the book. Begin reading, encouraging children to join you at any point. Reread the book, encouraging all children to choral read the book with you.

Show the handwritten version of the lyrics to the class. Tell children that these are the very same words that were in the book you just read. Using a pointer, point to each word as you and the class choral read the song again. Reinforce to the class that this is one form of reading, and that they just showed that they were, indeed, readers.

Supporting Children's Learning

Some children need multiple experiences "reading" the same song before they believe they can read it. Offer repeated experiences choral reading these charts as a whole class, reading the book or a printed version of the lyrics in small groups, and practicing reading the book or a printed version individually (with one child paired with a supportive adult—you, a parent, or an adult volunteer).

(KW) (1F) (2F)

Acting Out the Story

Lesson Target

To support children's comprehension of stories

Teacher Tip

Take a role in the dramatization for yourself. Especially when introducing acting out stories to children, it is sometimes helpful to model ways that a role can be dramatized.

Why Teach This

Children with different learning styles need different kinds of support to enhance their comprehension of what they read. Kinesthetic learners are more likely to remember different elements of a story that they have dramatized.

Secondary Objective

- To focus children's attention on the way language is often used in books, such as emphasizing repeated phrases as in "That Sam-I-Am, that Sam-I-Am, I do not

like green eggs and ham" from Dr. Seuss's *Green Eggs and Ham,* or giving characters special traits, like "poor Big Anthony" from Tomie dePaola's *Strega Nona* series.

Links to ELA Standards

- Students apply a wide range of strategies to comprehend, interpret, evaluate, and appreciate texts.
- Students participate as knowledgeable, reflective, creative, critical members of a variety of literacy communities.

Learning Materials

- a quality piece of children's literature (such as *Anansi and the Moss-Covered Rock* by Eric A. Kimmel [Holiday House, 1990] or a similar book)
- simple props to dramatize that particular story

Time Range

20–30 minutes

Before You Start

For the book *Anansi and the Moss-Covered Rock,* gather a large rock, a coconut, a banana, and a pineapple. Make large name tags for each character in the story, i.e., Elephant, Lion, Hippopotamus, Anansi, and Little Bush Deer.

Students' Prior Experience

Children need to have had many experiences listening to stories and discussing them.

To Do

Gather children in the group meeting area and have them sit in a large circle. Tell children that you will read them a story and that they should listen very carefully because the class will act out the story afterward. Read the book.

Ask children to list the characters so they will know how many children are needed to take part in the play. Use a fair way to assign parts to children (see "Teacher Tip" at right). Give each child the proper name tag and necessary props. Tell the rest of the class that they are the chorus, reading together the repeating phrases in the story, such as: *"…went walking, walking through the forest."*

Reread the story, nodding to each character when it is his or her turn to act. Repeat the story with different children taking on the characters' roles if time allows.

Supporting Children's Learning

For children who have difficulty remembering the plot of the story or the dialogue among the characters, start with very short stories or poems that offer every child a role to act. For example, read *The Very Hungry Caterpillar* by Eric Carle, asking all the children to pretend to be the caterpillar.

Teacher Tip

Try this idea for establishing a fair way to take turns. Label individual craft sticks with each child's name. Color one end of the stick to distinguish it. Place the sticks, colored end down, in a small cup. Pull a stick for each character in the story. When you replace the sticks in the cup, turn them so the colored ends are now showing. This way, the next time you need characters, you can easily pick new children without duplicating ones who have already had a turn.

Teacher Tip

Let children create their own masks using paper plates and craft sticks (or tongue depressors). Children who are shy or self-conscious about speaking in front of a group—especially English-language learners—find it easier to perform when they have a mask to hide behind. Encourage shy children to use puppets and stage an informal puppet show to dramatize a story.

Expanding the Lesson

It is not always necessary to act out entire stories, especially when children are reading long books or chapter books. Ask children to perform only one scene.

KF **1F**

Sorting by Letters

Lesson Target

To visually discriminate among letters so that a child can focus attention on just one letter

Why Teach This

Since children do not naturally attend to words at the letter level, this activity focuses their attention on the individual letters in words. Examining words letter by letter is an important skill for children to use when decoding unknown words.

Secondary Objective

- To reinforce children's association of letters to their sounds

Link to ELA Standards

- Students draw on their understanding of textual features (e.g., sound–letter correspondence, sentence structure, context, graphics).

Learning Materials

- nursery rhyme (or other poem, or the text of a familiar book)
- sentence strips
- pocket chart
- scissors
- butcher paper, long enough to be divided into 26 sections

Time Range

10–15 minutes

Before You Start

On a length of butcher paper, draw vertical lines to create 26 sections. Label each section with a letter of the alphabet (e.g., *Aa*, *Bb*, *Cc*, and so on). Write the selected nursery rhyme on sentence strips and place them in the pocket chart near the group meeting area. A good rhyme to start with is "One, Two, Buckle My Shoe."

Students' Prior Experience

Children have had two or three experiences with the "Being the Word" activity.

Expanding the Lesson

Possible Questions to Ask About Letters

- Which letters are used a lot of times?
- Which letters are used a few times?
- Which letters are not used at all?
- How many letters are used two times? three? four?
- Are any letters used the same number of times?
- Are there double letters (i.e., the same letter used side by side) in any words?
- Is the same letter used more than once in a word (i.e., letters used twice but not next to one another)?

One, Two, Buckle My Shoe

One, two,
Buckle my shoe.
Three, four,
Shut the door.
Five, six,
Pick up sticks.
Seven, eight,
Lay them straight.
Nine, ten,
A big fat hen.

To Do

Gather children in the group meeting area and have them sit in a large circle. Tell them that you will be reading a familiar nursery rhyme to them. Pointing to the words on the sentence strips, read the nursery rhyme aloud. Ask children to chorally read the nursery rhyme.

As children watch, cut the words apart and give each child a word. This action focuses children's attention on one word so they can then focus on each letter of that word. Explain to children that you are going to call out a letter of the alphabet. Tell children to look at their word carefully, and if their word has that letter in it, they should stand. Do this for a few letters until children get the concept of "looking for a letter inside the word."

A
lay; straight; a; fat

B
buckle; big

C
buckle; pick; sticks

D
door

E
one; buckle; shoe; three; three; the; five; seven; seven; eight; them; nine; ten; hen

F
four; five; fat

G
eight; straight; big

H
shoe; three; shut; the; eight; them; straight; hen

I
five; six; pick; sticks; eight; straight; nine; big

J

K
buckle; pick; sticks

L
buckle; lay

M
my; them

N
one; seven; nine; nine; ten; hen

O
one; two; shoe; four; door; door

P
pick; up

Q

R
three; four; door; straight

S
shoe; shut; six; sticks; sticks; seven; straight

T
two; three; shut; the; sticks; eight; them; straight; straight; ten; fat

U
buckle; four; shut; up

V
five; seven

W
two

X
six

Y
my; lay

Z

Next, call out another letter. As children stand, ask them to come to the butcher paper and write a tally mark under the letter that has been called. Explain that if their word has two of the same letter, they should make two tally marks under that letter. Slowly call out all the letters of the alphabet, making sure that children have enough time to make their tally marks before you call out the next letter.

Ask children to examine the butcher paper chart to find letters of the alphabet that were not used in any words. (In the nursery rhyme "One, Two, Buckle My Shoe" there are no words containing *J*, *Q*, or *Z*). Ask children to find the letter that was used the most times. (In this example, *E* was used 14 times.) Children will have to total the number of tally marks before doing this part of the activity. Use the chart on page 54 that lists each word in this nursery rhyme under all the letters of the alphabet to determine other questions to ask the class.

End the lesson by asking children to look at the letters as they read. Remind them that the letters have sounds and that those sounds make up the words.

◄ Expanding the Lesson ►

After children have had two or three opportunities to do this activity, modify the activity. Instead of making a tally mark, ask children to write their word under each letter that it contains. For example, the word *shoe* would be written under the *s*, *h*, *o*, and *e* columns. If the butcher paper is long enough, several children could work on the chart at the same time.

Supporting Children's Learning

If children have difficulty focusing on each letter in their word, have these children sit near you. When you call out a letter that is in one of their words, remind them to look at the word and check for that letter. After they have made a tally mark for a certain letter, ask them to cross out that letter. This way, they can focus their attention on their remaining letters when a letter is called. Or have children cut apart the letters in their word and glue the letter in the proper place on the chart. When choosing this option, allow enough space between letters for children to cut.

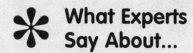

What Experts Say About...

Knowing Letter Names

• Letters should be introduced to children through a variety of materials: alphabet blocks, letter cards, board games, alphabet wall charts, and alphabet books.

• Preschool children who recognize some letters have an advantage when they enter school.

• A child's ability to name letters in kindergarten is the strongest predictor that he or she will be a competent reader by third grade.

Source: Burns, Griffin, & Snow, 1999

Individual & Partner Reading Activities

KF

Matching Capital Letters

Lesson Target
To visually discriminate among letters so that a child can match a set of magnetic letters with the appropriate letter shape

Why Teach This
Quality visual-discrimination skills help children immediately see the differences between words. The lowest level of visual-discrimination skill is distinguishing between letters. Competency at this level aids in children's reading success.

Secondary Objective
• To sequence letters in alphabetical order

Link to ELA Standards
• Students draw on their understanding of textual features (e.g. sound–letter correspondence, sentence structure, context, graphics).

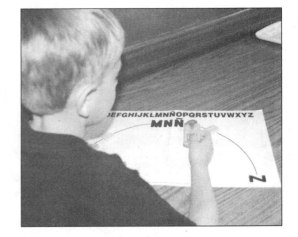

Learning Materials
• set of magnetic capital letters
• Activity Mat of Capital Letters (page 57)
• gallon-size reclosable plastic bags

Time Range
10–15 minutes

Before You Start
Identify children in the class who cannot yet recognize all letter names and/or need help discriminating one letter from another. Make copies of the Activity Mat of Capital Letters and laminate them for durability. Store sets of magnetic capital letters in plastic bags. Prepare enough sets of materials so that each pair of children has their own materials.

Students' Prior Experience
Working with a partner

A B C D E F G

H I J K L M N

O P Q R S T

U V W X Y Z

Teacher Tip

Children who have trouble matching the outline and magnetic letter will need more practice. Use one hand to point to the letter and one to point to the corresponding outline. Moving both hands together, trace the letter's form, discussing the matching qualities. For example, as you demonstrate this with a capital *N*, say: *I am starting both hands at the top and moving my fingers straight down. I stop here and move to the top again. Now I move my fingers down this slanted line, sliding them to the bottom. I stop here and move to the top again. Now I move straight down again, stopping at the bottom.*

To Do

Gather children who would benefit from this activity in the group meeting area. Ask them to sit in a circle on the floor. Put one activity mat on the floor where all children can see it. Point to the letters and encourage children to say the letter names (or sing "The Alphabet Song") with you.

Pull one letter from the plastic bag. On the mat, slide your finger over the letters until you reach the letter from the bag. Talk about the similarities between the letter on the activity mat and the letter you are holding. For example, if the letter is a capital *M*, say: *Both letters have four straight lines. The lines go up and down and up and down. Both of these letters are capital* M. Ask children if the letters match, then place the letter on the mat on top of the matching outline. Model two or three more letters.

Ask one child to pull a letter from the bag and find its match on the activity mat. Repeat two or three times. Explain to children that they are going to work in pairs to match all the letters in the bag to the letters on the activity mat. Distribute materials to pairs of children. Monitor partners as they work, encouraging them to orally describe the letters they are matching and to name them. When partners are finished matching all letters, ask them to point to and say all the letter names.

Ask children to return all magnetic letters in the plastic bag and put all the materials back where they belong.

Supporting Children's Learning

If children have difficulty matching capital letters with entire sets of magnetic letters, reduce the number of letters they work with, making sure that the letters are very different from one another, e.g., *B, C, H, M, O, S, U, X,* and *Z.*

KF 1F

Matching Capital Letters to Lowercase Letters

Lesson Target

To visually discriminate among letters so that a child can match lowercase letters to the appropriate capital letter

Why Teach This

Honing children's visual-discrimination skills helps them immediately see the differences between words. The lowest level visual-discrimination skill is distinguishing between letters. The next level of visual discrimination is matching capital and lowercase letters.

Secondary Objective
- To sequence letters in alphabetical order

Link to ELA Standards
- Students draw on their understanding of textual features (e.g. sound–letter correspondence, sentence structure, context, graphics).

Learning Materials
- set of magnetic letters, both capitals and lowercase
- Activity Mat of Capital Letters (page 57)
- gallon-size reclosable plastic bags
- alphabet chart with both capital and lowercase letters (Post the chart on the wall at children's-eye level so it can be seen from the group meeting area.)

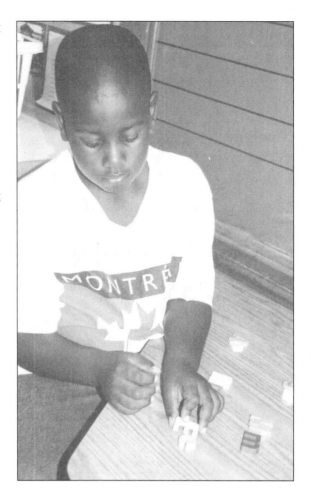

Time Range
10–15 minutes

Before You Start
Identify children in the class who need more practice matching capital and lowercase letters. Make copies of the Activity Mat of Capital Letters and laminate them for durability. Put sets of 52 magnetic letters (26 capital and 26 lowercase letters) in plastic bags. Prepare enough sets of materials so that each pair of children has their own materials.

Students' Prior Experience
Working with a partner

To Do
Gather children who would benefit from this activity in the group meeting area. Ask them to sit in a circle on the floor. Hold up one activity mat so all children can see it. Point to the capital letters and encourage children to say the letter names (or sing "The Alphabet Song") with you.

Place the activity mat on the floor where all children can see it. Take a bag and pour the letters on the floor. Sort capital letters into one pile and lowercase letters into another, making sure to put all letters flat on the floor where they can be seen.

Choose one capital letter. Using the mat, run your finger over the letters until you reach the chosen letter. Talk about the similarities between the letter on the activity mat and the letter you are holding. For example, if the letter is a capital *S*, say: *This letter is one long curvy line.* Put the capital *S* on the activity mat.

Ask one child to go to the alphabet chart and point to the capital *S*. Ask him to describe the lowercase letter beside it. Model scanning the group of lowercase letters to find the lowercase *s*, then place the lowercase letter below the capital *S* on the activity mat. Model the same procedure with two or three more letters.

Explain to children that they are going to work in pairs to put all the capital letters in the correct place on the mat and match all the lowercase letters to their capital letter. Distribute materials to pairs of children. Monitor partners as they work. When partners are finished matching all letters, ask them to point to and say all the letter names.

Ask children to return all magnetic letters in the plastic bag and put the materials back where they belong.

Supporting Children's Learning

Matching a lowercase letter to its capital letter is not a skill easily learned. For children who have difficulty with this activity, try giving each pair of children their own smaller version of an alphabet chart so they do not have to keep referring to the one on the wall. If they continue to experience problems, create activity mats with only a few letters on them and give children only the letters that are on the mat.

KF 1F

Sorting Words

Lesson Target

To show children how to pay attention to parts of words and compare words as they look for similarities (e.g., same initial letter, same rime, or a particular letter anywhere in the word)

Why Teach This

Successful word study for young children starts as children begin grouping words together by a particular attribute. This activity builds on the letter-study lessons previously introduced.

Secondary Objective

• To find rhyming words among a set of rhyming and non-rhyming words

Link to ELA Standards

• Students draw on their understanding of textual features (e.g. sound–letter correspondence, sentence structure, context, graphics).

Learning Materials

- pocket chart
- 3-by-5-inch index cards
- markers
- sandwich-size reclosable plastic bags

Time Range

10–15 minutes

Before You Start

Prepare a set of 20 word cards. On separate index cards, write ten words that rhyme and ten words that do not rhyme. (For example, *at, bat, cat, fat, hat, mat, pat, rat, sat, vat; bird, song, dress, pencil, book, apple, pear, shoes, socks, card.*) Prepare a separate

set of cards with the following headings: "Rhymes," "Does Not Rhyme," "Begins With /b/ Sound," "Does Not Begin With /b/ Sound." Store these cards in a small reclosable plastic bag. Have extra index cards and a marker nearby.

Students' Prior Experience

Children have had previous lessons in rhyming words and participated in many activities where they distinguished orally between words that rhyme and those that do not rhyme. Children also have participated in many activities where they distinguished orally between words that start with the same initial consonant and those that do not begin with the same sound.

To Do

Gather children in the group meeting area and ask them to sit in a large circle. Explain that today's new activity for reading choice time is called "Sorting Words."

Show the class the plastic bag. Take out the two heading cards that say "Rhymes" and "Does Not Rhyme." Put the "Rhymes" card in the top pocket of the pocket chart. Put the "Does Not Rhyme" card in a pocket halfway down the pocket chart. Point to each card as you read it.

Ask children to watch and listen carefully as you show them a card and read aloud the word on it. Explain that if the word rhymes with *-at*, they should show a thumbs-up sign, and the card will go in the pocket chart under the "Rhymes" heading. If the word does not rhyme with *-at*, they should show thumbs down, and the card will go under the "Does Not Rhyme" heading.

Show one rhyming-word card to the class and read the word aloud. When children show thumbs up, respond: *Right*, bat *rhymes with* -at. Ask a child to put that card in the correct place in the pocket chart. Each time you show a card, reinforce the lesson by repeating the sounds aloud in this manner.

Show the other cards, responding to children and asking different volunteers to put those cards in the correct place in the pocket chart. Explain that these cards will be in the reading center later for them to choose as an activity.

Next, explain to the class that they are going to create a different set of words to sort during reading-choice time. Ask children to close their eyes and think of a word that begins with the /b/ sound. Tell them that you need ten words that begin with *B*. Ask random children for their word and write the first ten on index cards. If a child mentions a word that does not begin with the /b/ sound, say something like: *No, that word begins with the /?/ sound. But I will also need ten words that do not begin with the /b/ sound, so I will write that word on a card anyway.*

When you have ten cards with words that begin with *B*, explain that you need to make ten (or however many more) cards for words that do not begin with the /b/ sound. Continue accepting words from children until you have enough cards.

Put the heading cards that say "Begins With /b/ Sound" and "Does Not Begin With /b/ Sound" in the pocket chart. Ask children to help you sort the cards by showing thumbs up to indicate if the word begins with the /b/ sound or thumbs down to indicate if the word does not.

Shuffle the cards and show them to children, reading the words one at a time. Ask different children to place each card under the correct heading. Then pick up all cards and place them in a small plastic bag. Explain that they can sort these two sets of word cards during reading-choice time. Add that they will be making more sets of word cards to sort.

TEACHING STRATEGIES

Criteria for Sorting Words

- Sort by same initial letter, using three different initial letters for children to sort

- Sort by same initial letter, using four different initial letters for children to sort

- Sort by same ending letter, using two different ending letters for children to sort

- Sort by same ending letter, using three different ending letters for children to sort

- Sort by same ending letter, using four different ending letters for children to sort

- Sort into two categories of same letter anywhere in the word

- Sort into two categories of same/not-same vowel sound (e.g., short-a sound and not short-a vowel sound)

- Sort into two categories of short/long vowel sound (e.g., short-a and long-a)

Supporting Children's Learning

If a child has difficulty determining under which category a word card should be placed, work with that child one-on-one. As children become accomplished at sorting cards into two categories, use additional sorting criteria listed in the "Teaching Strategies Box" at left.

KF **1F**

Collecting and Reading Environmental Print

Lesson Target
To reinforce children's view of themselves as readers

Why Teach This
"Reading" logos and other forms of environmental print supports young children's beliefs that they are readers. Even when children cannot read certain words conventionally, they can read them in the context of a logo, e.g., McDonald's®, Taco Bell®, Wendy's®, and so on.

Secondary Objective
• To sort recognizable words by their initial letter

Link to ELA Standards
• Students apply knowledge of language structure and language conventions to discuss print texts.

Learning Materials
• magazines, newspapers, coupons
• 26 sheets of 18-by-24-inch construction paper
• scissors
• glue sticks
• basket labeled "Logos"

Time Range
15–20 minutes

> ### Teacher Tip
> Young children tend to like this activity very much. Ask families to send logos to school so that there will be enough for children who choose this activity. See page 64 for a sample letter to send to families asking for their help.

Before You Start
Label 26 sheets of large construction paper with a letter of the alphabet (*Aa*, *Bb*, *Cc*, and so on). Post these in an area of the classroom that is low enough so that every child in the class can reach them. Collect several logos that are easily recognizable to children in your particular class and put them near the group meeting area. Label a small container "Logos" and put it in the reading center near a smaller basket with two or three glue sticks.

Students' Prior Experience
Children should have had many experiences identifying letter names and their accompanying sounds. Children should have had experiences working with a partner.

Collecting Logos

Dear Families:

We started a new activity today. If you come to the classroom, you'll see 26 sheets of construction paper posted on the walls. Each sheet of paper is labeled with a letter of the alphabet.

For the next few weeks, one of our reading choices will be sorting commercial logos and posting them on the correct sheet of paper. We'll need lots of logos for this activity; for example, McDonald's®, Kellogg's®, or Crest®. I would appreciate it if you could take a few minutes and work with your child to find some logos and cut them out.

You can cut the logos out of boxes, labels on cans of food, or bags from fast-food restaurants. You can also clip them from magazines, newspapers, or even grocery circulars. We have a new basket in the reading center, labeled "Logos," where children can put any logos brought to school.

When young children "read" logos, it helps them believe they are readers. Even if they cannot read those words in the adult way of reading, reading logos is real reading for young children. So, as you are cutting out logos for our class, ask your child to read the logos to you, and then talk about the first letter of the word and the sound that that letter makes.

Sincerely,

To Do

Gather children in the group meeting area. Show one logo to the class and ask children to read it. Say: *Say the word very slowly and listen to the first sound your mouth makes when you say this word. What letter makes that sound?* Acknowledge the correct answer. Show four or five other logos and repeat the question.

Point to the empty lettered pages and ask children to put each logo on the correct lettered paper. Call a child, ask her to choose a logo, name the first sound, and glue the logo to the correct lettered paper. Repeat for the other logos you showed earlier. Explain to children that this activity will be a reading-choice activity for the next few days (or weeks).

Ask children to look for logos at home in magazines, newspapers, grocery circulars, or on food packages or containers. Remind children not to cut out anything without first asking permission from their family. Ask children to cut out logos, bring them to school, and put them in the basket labeled "Logos" in the reading center. Show the class the basket and where it is stored.

Supporting Children's Learning

For children who have difficulty matching logos to the correct letter of the alphabet, make sure that the initial letter on the logo is very clear (not stylized in any way). Pair that child with one who completes this task with ease. Ask that partner to talk through the task as he or she does it.

TEACHING STRATEGIES

Activities That Engage Children With Environmental Print

- Bind 26 blank pages and a "Logos I Can Read" title page for each child in the class.

- Create an environmental-print learning center with magazines, catalogs, and newspapers for children to cut out logos that they can read. Put sorting mats into the center so children can sort logos according to where in the house these things might be found, e.g., pantry, refrigerator, bathroom, and so on.

- After the environmental alphabet chart has hung in the class for several weeks, take down the charts and bind into a class book.

KW **1F**

Using Magnetic Letters

Lesson Target

To teach how to use magnetic letters to create words

Why Teach This

Understanding the concept that words are created by combining several letters in a distinct order is basic to learning how to read. Reinforce this concept by giving children opportunities to practice putting letters in correct order to make familiar words.

Secondary Objective

- Learning to handle magnetic letters to make words leads to other successful activities with letters.

Link to ELA Standards

- Students apply knowledge of language structure and language conventions to discuss print texts.

Learning Materials

- several sets of magnetic letters, capital and lowercase
- 3 or 4 cookie sheets (or other flat, metal sheets)
- 3 or 4 clear storage containers (or shoeboxes)
- a variety of alphabet books
- index cards and sentence strips
- markers

Time Range

10–15 minutes

Before You Start

You may use regular shoeboxes for storing the magnetic letters, but clear containers with snap-on lids are less likely to spill. On index cards and sentence strips, carefully print words and simple sentences that are suitable for children to copy with the magnetic letters.

Students' Prior Experience

Working with a partner

Teacher Tip

For younger children, label spaces on shelves where they should return the materials. Each label could have a photograph of the material as well as a written word. Illustrations or photographs cut from catalogs can also label the space.

To Do

Gather children in the group meeting area. Show children the magnetic letters in their storage container, cookie sheets, and collections of word cards (or sentences written on sentence strip). Tell children that "Using Magnetic Letters" is a choice during reading-choice time. Demonstrate how the magnetic letters stick to the metal cookie sheet.

Show students several activities to do with the magnetic letters and cookie sheets. Possible activities include:

- Make your name.
- Make your partner's name.
- Make all the words that start with the letter *R* from the word wall (or that start with *C*, *D*, *E*, and so on).
- Make words with the same first letter (*red*, *run*, *rug*) or last letter (*hop*, *pop*, *cup*).
- Make color words, number words, animal names, and so on.

Demonstrate how to get the materials from the reading center (or wherever these materials are stored).

Choose one child as your partner. Ask the child to choose one word from the stack of word cards. Model making that word by slowly selecting one letter at a time, working from left to right. Talk aloud as you search through the magnetic letters using language, such as: *I am going to make the word* red. *The first letter I need to find is* R. *It is not this letter. That is an* S. *I am looking for a letter with a straight line on the left side. This is an* I. *I don't need it. This one has the right kind of line, but it is an* M. *This is the* R. *Now, I need to find an* E. At some point, ask your partner to help you find a particular letter. Next, choose two children to demonstrate how to do "Using Magnetic Letters."

Show children how to clean up the materials when finished (place the letters in the box, snap the lid on the box, put the box on the shelf, stack the cookie sheets so that they fit together, and so on).

Teacher Tip

Magnetic letters are relatively inexpensive and readily available in different types of stores. For children who need additional support learning to name the letters of the alphabet or remembering the sound associated with each letter, suggest that families purchase a set of magnetic letters. See page 69 for a sample letter to send to families offering specific activities they can do with their child using magnetic letters.

Expanding the Lesson

Some young children come to school having had very few experiences with letters of the alphabet. Some of these children would benefit from the simple visual-discrimination activity of matching magnetic letters to the appropriate letter shape on an activity mat. See pages 57 and 70 for reproducible activity mats to support this activity.

Supporting Children's Learning

Most young children remember this routine after the first demonstration. For those few children who have difficulty remembering the routine for "Using Magnetic Letters"—where the materials are stored, what their options are for words to make, or how to return materials to their proper place—talk the child through the routine as he performs the steps, or have him ask another student for assistance. You can also provide laminated lists or menus that document the choices for "Using Magnetic Letters" activities, like the one on page 68.

Menu of Magnetic Letter Activities

Pick one of the activities below to do
with magnetic letters:

- Make your name.

- Make your partner's name.

- Make words from the word wall,
  like all the words that start with *R*
  (or *C, D, E,* and so on).

- Make words with the same first letter
  (for example, *red, run, rug*).

- Make words with the same last letter
  (for example, *hop, pop, cup*).

- Make color words.

- Make number words.

- Make animal names.

 Scholastic Teaching Resources

Activities to Do With Magnetic Letters

Dear Families:

This week we have started working with magnetic letters. You might be surprised at how much your child has taken to something as simple as arranging magnetic letters on cookie sheets to make words!

I have provided alphabet books and words written on index cards for children to use as models for creating different words. When I introduced this activity, I suggested that children could do several things with the letters. You might suggest some of these same activities at home:

- Make your name.
- Make your partner's name.
- Make all the words from the word wall that begin with *R* (or *C, D, E,* and so on).
- Make words with the same first letter (e.g., *red, run, rug*) or last letter (e.g., *hop, pop, cup*).
- Make color words, number words, animal names, and so on.

Children are developing the concept that words are created through combining several letters in a distinct order. Help reinforce this concept by having your child practice putting letters in correct order to make familiar words. When children do the same kind of activities at home and at school, they learn reading concepts more quickly.

Working with magnetic letters should not be a long, time-consuming activity. Just spend 5 to 10 minutes a day on this activity. Your child can even do this while you prepare dinner. Put a set of magnetic letters on the refrigerator and talk with your child about making words while you are tossing a salad.

Thank you for working with your child at home.

Sincerely,

Activity Mat of Lowercase Letters

abcdefgh
ijklmnopq
rstuvwxyz

KW **1F**

Building Color Words

Lesson Target
To focus children's attention on specific letters that make certain words

Why Teach This
Young children learn best when engaged in concrete, hands-on activities. This is not always possible in the area of reading. Using cubes that snap together from the math area gives children another manipulative to use to create words. (These cubes can also be purchased in commercially prepared sets.)

Secondary Objective
- To add color words to children's sight-word vocabularies

Link to ELA Standards
- Students apply knowledge of language structure and language conventions to discuss print texts.

Learning Materials
- 7 sets of interlocking cubes
- fine-point permanent markers
- small reclosable plastic bag

Time Range
10–15 minutes

Before You Start
Create your own letter cubes by printing letters on interlocking cubes with a fine-point permanent marker. (Or you can purchase similar products, such as Unifix® Letter Cubes, which are commercially available.) You can also use alphabet stickers or small dot stickers with the letters written on them.

    For this lesson, each child needs a set of the following letters: *b, d, e, e, e, e, g, l, n, r, r, u*. These letters make the words *red*, *blue*, and *green*. If children will make different color words, you'll need other letters as well. Put each set of letters in a small reclosable bag.

Teacher Tip
You can use any style of interlocking cubes for this activity. Make sure that the cubes are large enough so children can easily see the letters.

Building the Color Words

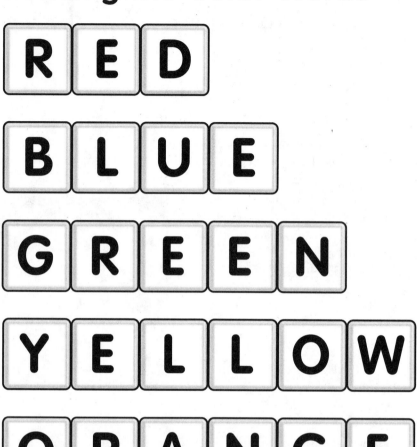

R E D

B L U E

G R E E N

Y E L L O W

O R A N G E

P U R P L E

B R O W N

B L A C K

Students' Prior Experience

Children need to have had previous experiences working in small groups and working with interlocking cubes.

To Do

Gather four to six children in the group meeting area. Explain that they will be working with interlocking cubes, but in a slightly different way than they do during math time.

Give each child a plastic bag with the interlocking letter cubes needed to make the words *red*, *blue*, and *green*. Ask children to organize the letter cubes on the floor in front of them, with each letter facing up.

Ask the group how to figure out how to spell the word *red*. Continue asking leading questions until one child suggests looking on a crayon, a marker, or a book with color words in it.

Ask one child to slowly read the letters in the word *red* to you. As the child says, *R-E-D*, snap an *E* onto the *R*, and a *D* onto the *RE*. Show the three-letter word to the group, and ask them to do the same thing.

Tell children that they have letters to make two more color words and that one of those words is *blue*. Ask children to find the word *blue* and copy it to make *blue* using the letter cubes. Do the same thing for the word *green*. Ask children to read the words with you.

Have children snap the cubes apart and return them to the correct bag.

Supporting Children's Learning

Children who understand this task can help others who are having difficulty. You can also give children a copy of "Building the Color Words" (page 72) so they do not have to find the color words or remember the spelling from a crayon or marker.

Sorting ABC Collections

Lesson Target

To teach children to sort objects by the beginning sound of their name

Why Teach This

Activities that specifically draw children's attention to letters, sounds, and words are useful to beginning readers. As children sort and match objects by the beginning sound of their names, children begin to internalize the letter sounds.

Secondary Objective

- To increase phonemic awareness

Link to ELA Standards

- Students draw on their understanding of textual features (e.g. sound–letter correspondence, sentence structure, context, graphics).

Learning Materials

- 26 small boxes of identical size and shape
- small objects with names that clearly represent their initial sounds

Time Range

10–15 minutes

Before You Start

Collect 26 small boxes with identical size and shape. (Boxes that checks are mailed in are ideal for this activity because they are sturdy and stack easily.) Cover the boxes with contact paper to make them even sturdier. Label each box with a letter of the alphabet, writing both the capital and lowercase letter.

Over time, collect at least four or five small items with names beginning with each letter of the alphabet. For example:

Cc: candle, car, caterpillar, comb, cork, corn, cow, cube, cup

Hh: hammer, hat, hazelnut, heart, horse, horseshoe

Pp: pencil, pen, penny, penguin, peppermint, pig, popcorn, porpoise

Tt: tangrams, tape, tea bag, top, toothbrush, toothpaste, towel

Students' Prior Experience

None

To Do

Gather children in the group meeting area and ask them to sit in a large circle. Show them the 26 small boxes, pointing out the letters written on each box. Tell children that these boxes are called "ABC Collections Boxes." Have four or five small objects at hand.

Show one object to class. Ask children: *What is this object called?* When children reach a consensus, ask: *In which box do you think this object should be stored?* When children answer correctly, give the object to a child and ask him to place the object inside the correct box. Repeat with the remaining objects.

> ### Teacher Tip
> Enlist students' families to help collect small items that represent letters of the alphabet. Send home a letter similar to the one on page 75, and keep families posted on the progress in number of items collected.

ABC Collections

Dear Families:

If you are willing, we are all going on a big scavenger hunt during our break. No, this does not mean that you have to go chasing around the school looking for items on a list. This is a different kind of scavenger hunt.

In class we are creating "ABC Collections Boxes." There will be 26 small boxes, one for each letter of the alphabet. Inside each box are small items that represent that letter/sound.

First, we need to gather 26 boxes—the kind that checks are mailed in. If you have any to spare, please send them to school with your child. Next, for each letter sound, we need items that are small enough to fit into these boxes. This is a challenge you and your child can work on together. Listed below are a few ideas for the first three letters, but do not feel limited to these objects. Search through your house and see what you and your family can locate. I'll bet the bottom of the toy box or the closet floor contains lots of small items like this:

"A" Collection Box Items
airplane, alligator, almond, anchor, apple, ant, audiotape

"B" Collection Box Items
ball, balloon, banana, bandage, battery, bay leaves, bird, boat, bolt, bottle, bow, bowl, box, bubbles, bubble bath, bulb, butterfly, button, bus

"C" Collection Box Items
camel, camera, can, candle, car, carrot, cashews, cat, caterpillar, cereal, circle, cocoon, comb, computer, cookie, cork, corn, cow, cube, cup

As you find these objects, talk with your child about their names, emphasizing their initial letter sounds. Send them to school after the break.

These collections will be great learning materials to add to our reading center. Sorting these collections will give children lots of practice listening for letter sounds.

Thanks for helping with this activity and for your continued support.

Sincerely,

Teacher Tip

As children become experts at sorting objects by initial letter sound, add boxes and objects that represent blends: *ch*, *sh*, *wh*, and *th*. Then include examples of both hard and soft *g* and *c*.

Explain to children that you are putting these ABC Collections Boxes in the reading center. Tell children that they can pour out the contents of two to four boxes at a time. They should choose one object, say its name, and listen carefully to its beginning sound. Then they should sort the objects back into their appropriate boxes. (As children become accomplished at this activity, increase the number of boxes that they can empty at any one time.)

Supporting Children's Learning

Initially some children will need support to pronounce the name of an object and hear the beginning sound. You can provide this support, or enlist the help of older—or more accomplished—children.

❋ What Experts Say About...

Using Manipulatives to Support Literacy Development

- Physically moving letter cubes or letter tiles helps young children focus on the letters that make up different words.

- Manipulatives especially support kinesthetic learners.

- Using letter tiles allows children to separate groups of letters and insert a space holder to indicate the syllables in words.

- Children need multiple experiences with letters before they internalize the letter names and sounds.

Sources: Allington, 2001; Taberski, 2000

Reading the Room

Lesson Target

To teach children how to read familiar words, signs, and charts in the classroom

Why Teach This

Beginning readers need multiple opportunities to be successful in reading. By building this success in simple ways, teachers prepare children to be successful readers. Reading the room helps children see themselves as readers.

Secondary Objectives

- To increase sight-word vocabulary

Links to ELA Standards

- Students read a wide range of print texts.
- Students use written language to accomplish their own purposes.

Learning Materials

- pointers
- readable print posted in the classroom (e.g., children's names on lockers, poems written on chart paper, word walls, and so on)

Time Range

10–15 minutes

Before You Start

Introduce this activity when you have sufficient print posted in the classroom. All print should be easy to read for children, either because the words are part of their sight-word vocabularies or because children had participated in posting the print. Examples of easily read print include children's names on lockers, poems written on chart paper, word walls, learning-center signs, words that label objects in the room (such as *door*, *chair*, *table*, and *window*), labels on book collections (such as *fiction*, *poetry*, and *Tomie dePaola books*), language experience stories, posters and charts made during other reading lessons, headings on bulletin boards, and alphabet charts.

Gather pointers and decide where to store them in the classroom. The pointers can be anything from yardsticks to "magic wands."

Students' Prior Experience

None

To Do

Gather children in the group meeting area. Write the phrase "Reading the Room" on chart paper. Explain that "Reading the Room" is a choice for partners during reading-choice time.

> ### Teacher Tip
>
> Offer a variety of pointers for children's use. Often, hardware stores will donate paint-stirring sticks for classroom use. You can also make pointers from new flyswatters. Cut out a word-size rectangle from the plastic end of the swatter. Children use this shape to outline the word they are reading. Glue a star (cut from iridescent paper) to the end of a dowel rod to make a "magic wand." Old radio or TV antennas can be recycled as telescoping pointers as well.

Show the pointers to children. Discuss safety issues, such as: point carefully, walk with the pointer turned down toward the floor, do not poke other children with the pointer, and return the pointers to where they belong when finished.

Choose a child to be your partner, then model walking around the room, pointing to various types of text, and reading the words quietly. When you've gone around the room once, ask your partner to "read the room." Assist the child if she needs help reading a word she has pointed to. Choose another set of partners and ask them to model "reading the room."

Remind children to return the pointers to their storage place when they are finished.

Supporting Children's Learning

Activities such as this encourage children to believe they can read and take more risks in reading. As children become adept at this activity in the room, they can go to other classrooms to "read the neighbor's room" as well. Arrange for your reading-choice time to be at the same time as nearby classrooms. Children from that class can come into your class to read while your students read that room. Or children whose behavior allows independent work can "read the hall" (or the office, computer lab, library, and so on).

KF **1F**

Reading the Alphabet Cards

Lesson Target

To teach children to associate one word for each letter of the alphabet

Why Teach This

Activities that specifically draw children's attention to letters, sounds, and words are useful to beginning readers. This activity reinforces children's ability to remember individual letter sounds while adding words to their sight-word vocabularies.

Secondary Objectives

- To increase phonemic awareness
- To increase sight-word vocabulary

Link to ELA Standards

- Students draw on their understanding of textual features (e.g., sound–letter correspondence, sentence structure, context, graphics).

Learning Materials

- a set of simple alphabet cards (one letter per card with an appropriate photograph and corresponding word, such as *Aa* with a picture of an apple and the word *apple*)
- gallon-size reclosable plastic bag

Time Range

10–15 minutes

Teacher Tip

Hang the alphabet cards low enough so they are at children's-eye level. Teachers often post alphabet cards very high on the wall, near the ceiling, making it difficult for children to interact with the cards.

Before You Start

Ensure that you have one card for each letter of the alphabet. Store the cards in a large reclosable plastic bag for student use or hang them in sequence on a wall.

Students' Prior Experience

None

To Do

Gather children in the group meeting area. Show the cards to children and explain that "Alphabet Cards" is one of the activities to choose during reading-choice time.

Model two or three of the following activities with the alphabet cards, asking children to join you:

- Read the chart as a choral reading (*A, a, apple; B, b, ball; C, c, cat*; and so on).
- Read every other card.
- Read only the letters.
- Read only the words.
- Read only the consonants.
- Read only the vowels.
- Name the pictures.
- Partner read the cards—the first child reads the name of the letter and the second child reads the word. Switch roles.
- Sing the cards.
- Cover selected letters with self-adhesive notes and have the partner guess the covered letter.
- One partner says the letter and the other points to it.
- Play "Guess the Letter"—one partner chooses a letter and gives clues to help the other child guess the letter. (For example: *It is in the middle, it has one hump, it is beside the letter* O.)

Supporting Children's Learning

If some children are having difficulty remembering the "Alphabet Cards" routine, pair them with more accomplished children who can model the routine and support the struggling child.

Expanding the Lesson

Create alphabet charts for children who need additional support in learning to name the alphabet or in remembering an anchor word for each letter. Reduce the alphabet cards on a photocopier and cut and paste the images so that all 26 letters/pictures/words fit onto an 8½-by-14-inch sheet of paper. Or, use the reproducible "Alphabet Chart" on page 80. Laminate the chart for durability. Send the alphabet chart home with these children along with a letter to families (see page 81 for a sample) explaining the activities they can do with their children to enhance letter learning.

Alphabet Chart

Aa apple	**Bb** ball	**Cc** cat	**Dd** dog
Ee egg	**Ff** fan	**Gg** goat	**Hh** hat
Ii igloo	**Jj** jump rope	**Kk** kite	**Ll** leaf
Mm moon	**Nn** nest	**Oo** orange	**Pp** pizza
Qq quilt	**Rr** ring	**Ss** sun	**Tt** turtle
Uu umbrella	**Vv** vest	**Ww** wagon	**Xx** x-ray
Yy yarn	**Zz** zipper		

Activities to Do With the Alphabet Chart

Dear Families:

Attached to this letter is an alphabet chart. You may want to spend a few minutes each night with your child doing some of the activities that we do in the classroom with this chart:

- Read the chart together (*A, a, apple; B, b, ball; C, c, cat*; and so on).

- Read every other letter.

- Read only the letters.

- Read only the words.

- Read only the consonants.

- Read only the vowels.

- Name the pictures.

- Partner read the chart—the adult reads the name of the letter and the child reads the word.

- Sing the cards—sing the ABC song while pointing to each letter as it is sung.

- Cover selected letters on the cards with self-adhesive notes and have the child guess the covered letter.

- The adult says the letter while the child points to it. Switch roles.

- Play "Guess the Letter"—the adult chooses a letter and gives clues to help the child guess the letter. (For example: *It is in the middle, it has one hump, it is beside the letter* O.)

These activities will help your child learn the names of letters and other important information about the alphabet.

Sincerely,

KF **1F**

Listening to a Book on Audiotape

Lesson Target
To teach children how to listen to a book on tape to help focus their attention and offer multiple times to practice connecting letters, sounds, and words with meaning

Why Teach This
Listening to books on tape is a lifelong skill. Adults often listen to audiotapes while driving or doing other activities. Recorded selections offer children a variety of book choices. Books on tape also expand children's imaginations as they incorporate sound effects, background sounds, rising or falling musical selections, and so on.

Secondary Objectives
- Repeatedly listening to a variety of books on tape expands children's familiarity with books, authors, and genres.
- Repeatedly listening to the same book offers children needed repetitive practice of reading skills.

Links to ELA Standards
- Students read a wide range of print and nonprint texts to build an understanding of texts.
- Students apply a wide range of strategies to comprehend, interpret, evaluate, and appreciate texts.

Learning Materials
- tape recorder
- piece of quality children's literature
- audiotape of same book

Time Range
5–15 minutes

Before You Start
Choose a favorite book of the class with an audiotape (professionally made or teacher created). This can be any book that is a favorite read-aloud of the class or a book used to support science or social studies instruction.

Students' Prior Experience
Children should have had several experiences with whole-group read-alouds and with making decisions with a classmate.

To Do

Gather children in the group meeting area. Begin by saying something like: *Some children have asked to hear certain books again and again, but there is not enough time during the school day to read books that many times. You know that you can sometimes check a book out and ask a parent or older sibling to read it to you. Now there will be a new choice for reading-choice time to help with this issue.* Show the class the tape recorder along with a book and the book on tape. Demonstrate how to put the tape into the tape recorder. Explain the buttons on the recorder. Push the "play" button and hold up the book so all children can see its front cover. Turn the pages as the signals on the tape indicate. When the tape finishes, demonstrate how to press the "stop" button and the "rewind" button.

Explain that listening to books on audiotape will be a reading choice from now on. Show children where the tape recorder (with headphones if possible, remembering to demonstrate how to connect the headphones to the tape recorder) will be kept. Explain how many book choices there will be and how partners should decide which book to listen to.

Supporting Children's Learning

Children who have not yet learned to track words across the page from left to right benefit from listening to tapes of very simple books. Since these are not usually available commercially, make them yourself. On each page, draw a star (or other familiar symbol) on the left side to indicate the beginning point of the text. Be very specific as you create the tape, instructing children to point to the star and touch each word. Remind children again and again to move from left to right to establish the idea of tracking. As you record slightly longer books, record directions to tell the listener when to make the return sweep as well.

CHAPTER THREE

For Early Readers

Overview

Young children move from the emergent stage of reading to the early reader stage when they begin to actually read small books. The definition of "reading" changes from context to context. Here, early readers are actually recognizing words, not merely saying the words that are on a page of text. (Emergent readers, on the other hand, memorize the text on a page because they have had multiple read-alouds with that text.)

Early readers are learning to use sounds automatically and to combine sounds to form the words that are on the page. While "sounding out" is still a major strategy, early readers discover other strategies to use. They are building a sight-word vocabulary and realizing that they do not have to sound out a word that they have memorized.

With early readers, instruction focuses on showing children how to use the skills they have recently learned. That is, this is the time children apply their learning to actually decode words, learning the process of reading. Careful scaffolding of the learning helps expand and build on what children have learned while reinforcing and solidifying these emergent skills.

Checklist of Signs of Early Readers

☐ **1.** Child looks like a reader by the way he holds a book and turns the pages.

☐ **2.** Child writes at the early writing stage of developmental (or invented) spelling, in which the child uses letters that represent sounds that she hears.

☐ **3.** Child recognizes several high-frequency words, along with words that have personal importance or relevance.

☐ **4.** Child names all of the letters in the alphabet and knows most of the sounds associated with letters.

☐ **5.** Child begins to recognize blends and digraphs and knows how to pronounce them.

☐ **6.** When one word is repeated several times in a story, child begins to recognize that word before the end of the story.

Strategies for Early Readers

KS **1F** **2F**

Making Connections

Lesson Target

To help children think about and discuss how parts of a text relate to something in their own lives

Why Teach This

Children constantly look for connections between what they already know and what they are learning. So it makes sense that when children bring past experiences to their reading, their reading comprehension increases. Pointing out these connections helps the learning process along.

Secondary Objective

• To bring background experiences to the reading process

Links to ELA Standards

• Students gather, evaluate, and synthesize data from a variety of sources.
• Students participate as knowledgeable, reflective, creative, critical members of a variety of literacy communities.

Learning Materials

• a short book about a young child

Time Range

20–25 minutes

Before You Start

Look for a book about a young child's experiences, such as Mercer Mayer's *All By Myself* (Golden Books, 2001). This book will help children easily connect similarities between the character's life and their own lives. See "Expanding the Lesson" at right for more suggestions.

Expanding the Lesson

These books by Mercer Mayer are good for helping children make text-to-self connections:

Just Me and My Dad (Golden Books, 2001)

Just Me and My Mom (Golden Books, 2001)

Just Grandpa and Me (Golden Books, 2001)

Just Grandma and Me (Golden Books, 2001)

Me and My Little Brother (Golden Books, 1998)

Me and My Little Sister (Golden Books, 1986)

Just My Friend and Me (Golden Books, 2001)

When I Get Bigger (Golden Books, 1999)

Books that have settings in schools help children make text-to-self connections, especially when they address emotional issues such as the first day of school or making friends. Suggestions include:

Chrysanthemum by Kevin Henkes (Greenwillow, 1991)

Friends at School by Rochelle Bunnett (Star Bright, 1995)

Lilly's Purple Plastic Purse by Kevin Henkes (Greenwillow, 1996)

Look Out Kindergarten, Here I Come! by Nancy Carlson (Puffin, 2001)

Tiptoe Into Kindergarten by Jacqueline Rogers (Cartwheel, 2003)

Will I Have a Friend? by Miriam Cohen (Aladdin, 1989)

Students' Prior Experience

Children have had multiple experiences listening to a variety of fictional stories and have been involved in group discussions about different aspects of these stories.

To Do

Gather children in the group meeting area. Tell children that for today's read-aloud, you will be reading about a character that is very much like the children in this class. Ask children to think about what they can do that the character could do. (If you are using *All By Myself*, explain that Little Critter is growing up and learning to do all kinds of things by himself. Ask children to think about how they are growing up and to consider what they can do that Little Critter can do.)

Read a few pages of the book, then ask: *Have you ever said the things that this character is saying?* Read a few more pages and repeat the question (or ask a similar one, such as: *Can you do what the character is doing?* or *Have you learned to _____ yet?*).

Finish reading the book, then ask children what happened in the book that reminded them of themselves. Listen to two or three children's comments as a group, then ask children to turn to a partner and share their connections. This way, everyone in the class gets an opportunity to tell their connection.

Explain to children that making connections to their own lives is something that the class is going to work on during read-alouds for the next few days.

Supporting Children's Learning

If children have trouble making text-to-self connections during whole-group sessions, work with them in small groups of four or five children. Try using a book that talks about young children in school-related stories, such as those listed in "Expanding the Lesson," page 85. When you use books set in a school environment, it is easier to know how events each child has experienced in the class relate to events in the book.

TEACHING STRATEGIES

Making More Connections

Text-to-self connections are the easiest connections for children to make. As children become competent at text-to-self connections, lead them in learning to recognize text-to-text and text-to-world connections.

When teaching text-to-text connections, help students make connections:

- within a series;
- in the same genre;
- about the same author's style;
- about the illustrator's techniques or choice of artistic medium;
- about the same character or similar characters;
- on the same topic or theme;
- about children in the same age group.

Strategies adapted from Fountas & Pinnell, 2001 and Keene & Zimmermann, 1997

KW **1F** **2F**

Figuring Out Unknown Words

Lesson Target
To reinforce strategies children can use to decode unknown words

Why Teach This
Many young children simply stop reading when they encounter a word that they do not recognize. They often look to an adult to tell them what the word is. This sense of helplessness can be overcome when children are taught different strategies to use as they encounter these words and are given multiple opportunities to practice these strategies.

Secondary Objective
• To review letter, blend, and digraph sounds

Links to ELA Standards
• Students gather, evaluate, and synthesize data from a variety of sources.
• Students apply a wide range of strategies to comprehend, interpret, evaluate, and appreciate texts.

Learning Materials
• "Reading Strategies" bookmarks (page 88)
• familiar picture book with some complex words (for example, Eric Carle's *The Very Hungry Caterpillar*)

Time Range
20–25 minutes

Before You Start
Photocopy the "Reading Strategies" bookmarks on card stock for each child. List words to use in this lesson that can be decoded using the strategies on the bookmark. If using *The Very Hungry Caterpillar*, consider these words: *leaf, butterfly*, and *Saturday*. (Children may be familiar with these words because they are so familiar with this book. Still, these words could be used as examples for what to do when they encounter a word they do not know.)

Students' Prior Experience
Children know the sounds associated with most letters, blends, and digraphs.

To Do
Gather children in the group meeting area. Explain that you will be looking at a book that everyone in the class knows very well. Turn to the first page of text, reading: *In the light of the moon, a little egg lay on a leaf.* Ask children: *How might*

Reading Strategies Bookmarks

Strategies to Figure Out an Unknown Word

- Look at the pictures.
- Use the initial letter of the word.
- Think about what would make sense in that sentence.
- Look through the whole word.
- Look for parts of words in the unknown word.
- Say, "Skip," and keep reading, then return to the beginning of the sentence.

Strategies to Figure Out an Unknown Word

- Look at the pictures.
- Use the initial letter of the word.
- Think about what would make sense in that sentence.
- Look through the whole word.
- Look for parts of words in the unknown word.
- Say, "Skip," and keep reading, then return to the beginning of the sentence.

Strategies to Figure Out an Unknown Word

- Look at the pictures.
- Use the initial letter of the word.
- Think about what would make sense in that sentence.
- Look through the whole word.
- Look for parts of words in the unknown word.
- Say, "Skip," and keep reading, then return to the beginning of the sentence.

Strategies to Figure Out an Unknown Word

- Look at the pictures.
- Use the initial letter of the word.
- Think about what would make sense in that sentence.
- Look through the whole word.
- Look for parts of words in the unknown word.
- Say, "Skip," and keep reading, then return to the beginning of the sentence.

you figure out the word leaf *if you could not read it?* Guide children into saying, *Look at the illustrations,* and *Use the initial letter of the word.* Explain to children that these are just a couple of strategies readers use when they have trouble figuring out unknown words.

Distribute the bookmarks to children. Read the title of the bookmark and the first two strategies. Explain to children that they will keep this bookmark with them during independent reading time to remind them of strategies to use to figure out unknown words. Read the other strategies aloud, asking children to follow along with you as you read.

Turn to the last page of *The Very Hungry Caterpillar* that says: *…he was a big beautiful butterfly.* Ask children what strategies they might use if they did not know the word *butterfly.* Lead them to suggest the strategy of looking for little words in the unknown word. Show children that they know the word *butter* and the word *fly,* so figuring out this word would not be difficult.

Next, turn to the page describing what the caterpillar ate on Saturday. Show children how they know the word *day.* Point out that if they look at the initial letter of the word and think about the days of the week, the word would have to be either *Saturday* or *Sunday.* If they look through the word, they would realize that it could not be *Sunday.*

Say: *As you can see, you can use more than one strategy to figure out an unknown word. I want you to try out these different strategies in your independent reading every day.*

Supporting Children's Learning

Some children will have difficulty using so many strategies. If you notice this, identify books with words that can be figured out using just one strategy. Work one-on-one with children or with small groups, adding new strategies only after they are using one strategy well.

TEACHING STRATEGIES

Strategies That Good Readers Use to Figure Out Unknown Words

- Look at the illustrations.
- Use the initial letter of the word.
- Think about what would make sense in that sentence.
- Look through the whole word.
- Look for parts of words in the unknown word.
- Say, "Skip," and keep reading, then return to the beginning of the sentence.

Whole- and Small-Group Reading Activities

KS **1F** **2F**

Reading News of the Day

Lesson Target

To focus children's attention on the skills used when spoken words are written down. Use "News of the Day" to help children apply the reading skills they are

learning. The specific targeted skill/concept for "News of the Day" will vary from day to day. Depending on what children dictate, the target may be initial letter sounds, high-frequency words, blends, and so on.

Why Teach This

Experts agree that children learn to read those things that mean something to them more quickly than any other type of text. What could be more meaningful to children than their own "News of the Day"? Every day children will dictate the "News of the Day." Children hear their friends say these words. They hear you repeat the words. They see you write the words. Then they try reading the words together. They take a copy of "News of the Day" home and read it to their family or listen to a family member read it to them. This routine provides daily support to a child learning to read.

Secondary Objective

• To increase children's sight-word vocabularies

Teacher Tip

Sending home copies of the "News of the Day" enhances the teaching/learning value of this activity. However, families may not realize their role in the learning process of their child. A sample letter explaining how they should interact with their child and "News of the Day" is provided on page 93.

Links to ELA Standards

• Students read a wide range of print and nonprint texts to build an understanding of texts.
• Students apply knowledge of language structure and language conventions to discuss print texts.
• Students participate as knowledgeable, reflective, creative, critical members of a variety of literacy communities.

Learning Materials

• transparency of News of the Day (page 91)
• dry-erase or transparency markers
• overhead projector
• copying machine
• copy paper

News of the Day

Day: _____ Date: _____

_____ said, _____

_____

_____

_____ said, _____

_____

_____

_____ said, _____

_____

_____

_____ said, _____

_____

_____

Time Range
15–20 minutes

Before You Start
Prepare a transparency of the "News of the Day" reproducible. Put the transparency and different colors of transparency markers near the overhead projector. Decide how children will take turns sharing their news of the day. See the "Teacher Tip" on page 52 for a suggestion.

Students' Prior Experience
Children know routines for group meetings and for taking turns talking.

To Do
Gather children in the group meeting area. Ask them to sit where they can see the screen on which the "News of the Day" will be projected. Explain to the class that you will be collecting news from four different children every day and writing their news on the transparency overhead.

Ask the class: *What day is today?* Write the day on the first line. Then ask: *What is today's date?* If necessary, refer to the class's calendar to locate the date. Write the date on the second line.

Ask one child: *What is your news today?* After the child answers, repeat her sentence, then write her name and sentence slowly, repeating each word as you write it. For example, Kathleen's news that "my cat had five kittens" would be written as: *Kathleen said, "My cat had five kittens."* Repeat with three more children, recording their news each time.

Reread the entire form, pointing to the text as you read. Invite children to join in the rereading as well. Make copies of the "News of the Day" and distribute them to children. Encourage children to read the "News of the Day" to their families at home.

Supporting Children's Learning
Because of the nature of this learning experience, different children will be reminded of different concepts within this lesson. As you reinforce the initial sounds in the word you are writing, the emergent reader gets a reminder of the sounds; the early reader gets a reminder about how letter sounds blend into words; and the independent reader gets a reminder about using descriptive words as you point out how *five* tells us how many kittens or how *loose* describes a tooth.

Expanding the Lesson

Give children a folder or binder to hold their copies of the "News of the Day" to create a meaningful diary of the class's experiences and record of their growth as readers. Early in the year, the comments and notations you make in the margins will relate to simpler skills and concepts than those found at the end of the year. Make it a part of each child's homework responsibilities to place the current day's page in the binder. To help foster accountability, ask children to bring their binders to school every once in a while to be checked.

Consider updating the "News" transparency as children's skill levels change. Add features such as "Joke of the Day," "Book of the Day," weather, upcoming events, and deadlines. You can also use the margins of the page to jot reminders (e.g., *Children are counted as tardy when they arrive after 8:00*), pleas for help (*We need adults to go with us to the zoo next Friday morning*), requests for materials (*Please send old magazines to school*), lists, and so on.

Explaining "News of the Day"

Dear Families:

Starting next Monday, I will be sending home our class's "News of the Day." At the end of every day, different children dictate one sentence apiece. I write that sentence on our special "News of the Day" form, then read it to the class. After four sentences, we reread the sentences as a class. So your child will have heard the sentences at least three times.

Reading the "News of the Day" to you offers your child another chance to read independently. Use it to spark conversation about events in your child's friends' lives or what goes on at school. At times, I'll use it as an opportunity to teach a particular skill. You'll see the notes that I make on the paper. I'll try to write enough so that you can reinforce this skill as well. Additionally, I sometimes jot a quick reminder on the "News" that you'll want to see.

Some families have found it meaningful to keep these pages in a three-ring binder. At the end of the year, you'll have a diary of our class's activities.

Thank you for helping and supporting your child's learning.

Sincerely,

Comparing Books by One Author

Lesson Target

To help children develop the understanding that real people write books

Why Teach This

Young children tend to think of books as somewhat magical, that they merely exist. For them to begin to think of themselves as readers and writers, it helps for them to understand that real people write the words and draw or paint the illustrations in picture books.

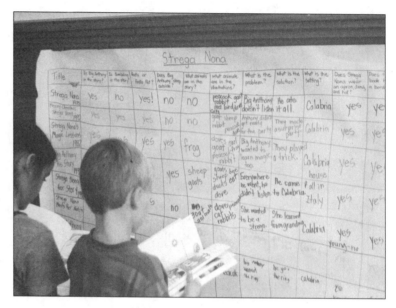

Secondary Objective

• Appreciating the fact that each author writes in his or her own style leads young children to develop their own writing style.

Links to ELA Standards

• Students apply a wide range of strategies to comprehend, interpret, evaluate, and appreciate texts.
• Students gather, evaluate, and synthesize data from a variety of sources.
• Students participate as knowledgeable, reflective, creative, critical members of a variety of literacy communities.

Learning Materials

• 5 books by the same author
• large chart paper or sheet of bulletin-board paper
• markers

Time Range

25–30 minutes per day for five consecutive days

Before You Start

Select five books by one author (for example, Eric Carle's *The Very Hungry Caterpillar*, *The Very Busy Spider*, *The Very Quiet Cricket*, *The Grouchy Ladybug*, and *The Very Lonely Firefly*). On a large piece of bulletin-board paper, draw a chart with six rows and six columns. Label the columns: "Title of the Book," "Author," "Illustrator," "Main Characters," "Setting," and "Plot."

Students' Prior Experience

Children need to have had many experiences listening to stories and discussing them.

To Do

Gather the class around the chart and read the headings to children. Explain that each day this week, the class will read a different book by Eric Carle (or whichever author you chose). Tell children to listen very carefully to the story so that at the end of the book, they can dictate the title of the book, its author and illustrator, the main characters, the setting, and the plot.

Read the first book. Ask children: *What is the title of the book?* Write their answer in the correct space of the chart. Next, ask: *Who is the author of the book?* Record their answer in the chart. Continue by asking the name of the illustrator, then the main characters, the setting, and the plot of the book. Write children's answers in the corresponding spaces on the chart. With the class, reread that day's entries.

Over the next few days, repeat this process with the other books. Discuss how the books are similar and how they are different. Ask questions such as:

- *Are the characters the same in all of the books?*
- *Does the author start his/her books the same way?*
- *Do all of the books have the same kind of ending?*
- *Does the author use the same setting for all the books?*
- *Is there a problem in each of the books?*
- *How does the author solve the problem?*

Expanding the Lesson

Introduce children to the special features that some authors use. For example, Marc Brown includes the names of his children (Tolon, Tucker, and Eliza) in his illustrations; Mercer Mayer often has spiders, crickets, or mice in his; and Tomie dePaola often includes a peacock, a white bird, or hearts. Record these on the chart after children have become more familiar with the process.

Supporting Children's Learning

To focus children's attention on how the books are similar, display the books near the chart. This way, children do not have to remember the previous day's book—they see it next to the chart. This gives less-capable children an extra reminder about the lesson's focus.

Individual & Partner Reading Activities

(KW)

Reading the Poetry Binder

Lesson Target
To reinforce young children's belief in themselves as readers

Why Teach This
Many young children view reading as something difficult; that is, too difficult for them to attempt. When they can look at a page full of words and say those words, they begin to see themselves as readers. Even when they cannot read those same words out of context, they still see themselves as reading the words they have memorized and can recite.

Secondary Objective
• To increase children's sight-word vocabularies

Link to ELA Standards
• Students read a wide range of print and nonprint texts to build an understanding of texts.

Learning Materials
• 1-inch 3-ring binder
• copies of familiar poems/lyrics to songs

Time Range
10–15 minutes

> ### Teacher Tip
> As children learn the lyrics to songs, type the lyrics using a large font and print a copy for the Poetry Binder.

Before You Start
Label a 1-inch 3-ring binder as the "Poetry Binder." Begin by including three or four familiar poems or songs that children have memorized.

Students' Prior Experience
Children need to have had experiences choral-reading poems.

To Do
Gather children in the meeting area and show them the binder you have prepared. Point to the title, reading the words "Poetry Binder." Explain to the class that this is a special binder where the class keeps copies of the poems and songs they memorize.

Show the first poem in the binder to the class and ask them to chorally read it. Point to the words as the class reads the poem. Repeat with the next poems.

Explain that partners can chorally read the Poetry Binder as a choice during reading time. Model what this choice should look like. Choose one child to be your partner. Sit on the floor next to each other, placing the binder on the floor in front of both of you. Turn to the first poem and read the poem with the child, pointing to the words as you read. Ask the child to choose another poem and read that poem together, again pointing to the words.

Put the Poetry Binder in the reading center where it will be kept.

Supporting Children's Learning

Be sure to include a variety of poems in the binder to meet the varying needs of all children. Some short, simple poems (or perhaps familiar nursery rhymes) will ensure success for less-capable students. Add rebus drawings over words that might be particularly difficult.

KW 1F

Working With Names

Lesson Target

To build on children's ability to recognize their own names and support them as they learn to recognize the names of their classmates

Why Teach This

Learning to read their names and their classmates' names helps children see themselves as readers. This begins in "Taking Attendance" (page 28). "Working With Names" extends children's ability to read others' names into the ability to create (with manipulatives) and write these names.

Secondary Objectives

- To focus children's attention at the letter level of words
- To reinforce children's understanding of letter–sound correspondence

Link to ELA Standards

- Students apply knowledge of language structure and language conventions to discuss print texts.

Learning Materials

- magnetic letters
- magnet board (or cookie sheet)

Teacher Tip

Few families realize how important names are to young children. Consider sending home the sample letter on page 99 to explain this concept to families. This encourages their involvement in supporting their children's reading development as they play some of the name games played at school.

- white board
- dry-erase markers
- sentence strips
- pocket chart

Time Range
10–15 minutes

Before You Start
Select names of children to use in this lesson and find magnetic letters to create these names. When first introducing this activity, use children's names with obvious similarities, such as 3-letter names, 4-letter names, and so on. Write the names on individual sentence strips, cut to size. Put the sentence strips in the pocket chart as well as labels that indicate the number of letters in names.

Students' Prior Experience
Children have been introduced to routines for group meetings and taking turns talking. Children have also had experience working with magnetic letters.

To Do
Gather children in the group meeting area and ask them to sit in a large circle. Explain to the class that you will be introducing a new reading choice, which is sorting the names of people in the class.

Using a large cookie sheet and magnetic letters, create the name of one child in the class. (Start with a two- or three-letter name if possible.) Ask: *How many letters are in this name?* Point out the one-to-one correspondence of the name written in magnetic letters with the one written on the sentence strip. Then place the sentence strip in the appropriate place in the pocket chart. Continue with three other children's names.

When finished, note the number of letters in each name, pointing out the similarities (number of letters, beginning or ending sound, and so on) in the names.

Supporting Children's Learning
Pair children who are having difficulty with this task with children who sort names easily.

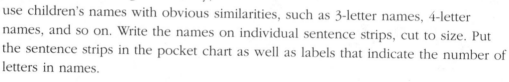

TEACHING STRATEGIES

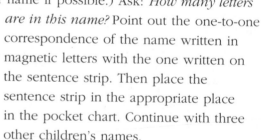

Working With Names

Children like working with their names and the names of their classmates. As children choose "Working With Names" less often, change this choice to other ways of working with names. Name activities include:

- sorting classmates' names according to the number of syllables in the name;
- matching name cards to picture cards of objects that begin with the same letter as children's names;
- adding names of people that everyone in the class knows, such as the principal, vice-principals, other teachers, nurse, library staff, cafeteria staff, and custodial staff.

A letter from your child's teacher

Working With Names

Dear Families:

Names are important as young children learn to read and write. You may have already noticed that one of the first words a child learns to read and write is his or her own name. Following that, young children usually become interested in learning about the names of people in their family and the names of their classmates.

Some of the activities we are doing with names during reading-choice time are:

- sorting classmates' names according to the number of syllables each name has—you could do the same thing with your child at home, using names of family members.

- matching name cards to picture cards of objects that begin with the same letter as children's names. Using pictures from magazines or catalogs, you and your child could make a set of cards to play this matching game. First, look for a picture of something that starts with *M*, such as a monkey, map, marble, marker, marshmallow, or motorcycle. Cut it out and glue it onto an index card. Write *Mother* on another index card. Continue making matching sets of cards like this for all family members.

- sort names by the number of letters in each name. You could do this with the names of people in your extended family.

By working on activities like this, your child will learn to pay more attention to details in words—an important skill in becoming an accomplished reader.

Sincerely,

KS **1W** **2F**

Reading With a Partner

Lesson Target
To give children an audience as they practice oral reading

Why Teach This
Children need practice reading aloud, but teachers never have enough time to listen to all children read every day. Most children do not like to read aloud alone, and reading one paragraph (or page) or every sixth paragraph (as in round-robin reading) gets boring. Partner reading provides a real audience for oral reading and keeps children actively involved in reading activities.

Secondary Objective
• To support children's ability to read with fluency and expression

Links to ELA Standards
• Students apply knowledge of language structure and language conventions to discuss print texts.
• Students read a wide range of print and nonprint texts to build an understanding of texts.

Learning Materials
• large selection of books at different reading levels
• basket labeled "Books for Partner Reading"

Time Range
10–15 minutes

Before You Start
Choose one book to use for modeling partner reading. Gather a sufficient number of books for children to choose from and put them in a basket labeled "Books for Partner Reading."

Students' Prior Experience
Children have had several experiences reading aloud to you.

To Do
Gather children in the group meeting area. Explain that you will be modeling a new activity for reading choices called "Partner Reading." Explain that partner reading is when two people select a book that they can read, then sit close together and read to each other, one at a time.

Ask one child to find a book that she can already read. Have her bring the book to the group meeting area. Sit on the floor beside the child and model how partners read to each other. Make sure you look at the book as the child reads to you, and point this out to the class.

Tell children that they will practice partner reading today. Ask children to choose a partner. Tell the class that each person needs to choose a book they can read, then find a place where both partners can sit side-by-side to read to each other. When both partners finish reading their books, they should put the books back where they belong and return to the group meeting area. Make sure children have something to do when they return to the group meeting area, so they are not just sitting and waiting for other partners to finish reading to each other.

Dismiss partners from the group area a few at a time to select books to read to each other.

Supporting Children's Learning

When children seem to have difficulty with partner reading, act as their partner once or twice to make sure they understand the expectations for this activity. If they continue having trouble, pair them with children who can be role models instead of allowing them to choose their own partner.

KW **1F** **2F**

Working With Word Families

Lesson Target
To help children readily recognize onsets and rimes

Why Teach This
One important reading strategy relates to patterns in words—recognizing patterns and decoding unfamiliar words that contain a known pattern. The simplest patterns to recognize are words that rhyme and have the same rime; for example, *bat*, *cat*, and *rat*. Each of these words rhymes and have the same *-at* rime. When a child knows most of the consonant sounds and recognizes the *-at* pattern, he can read many other words, such as *mat*, *fat*, and *hat*.

Secondary Objectives
• To reinforce children's ability to hear and create rhyming words
• To increase children's sight-word vocabularies

Link to ELA Standards
- Students apply knowledge of language structure and language conventions to discuss print texts.

Learning Materials
- magnetic letters
- magnet board
- chart tablet
- markers

Time Range
10–15 minutes

Before You Start
Before teaching the first lesson on word families, create a list of word-family rimes to teach to the class. (See "Expanding the Lesson," page 103.) Place the rimes in the order you want to introduce them to the class. Create a list of onsets for each rime to make real words.

Students' Prior Experience
Children have been introduced to routines for group meetings and for taking turns talking.

✳ What Experts Say About...

Phonological Awareness

- Children demonstrate their phonological awareness by noticing rhymes, making up silly names for things by substituting one sound for another, clapping syllables in a long word or a phrase, or commenting that several words begin with the same letter sound.

- Children learn initial phonological awareness skills through songs, rhyming games, and poems.

- A strong sense of phonological awareness in kindergarten and first grade predicts competent readers by third grade.

Source: Burns, Griffin, & Snow, 1999

To Do
Gather children in the group meeting area. Put the letters *C*, *A*, and *T* on the magnet board and ask children to read the word. Say: *Do you know that when you can read the word* cat, *you can read lots of other words, too? That's because when you read* cat, *you know what* /-at/ *sounds like.* Write the word *cat* on chart paper and ask children to read the word again.

On the magnet board, remove the *C* and put a *B* in its place. Ask children to read this word. Explain that /-at/ sounds exactly the same in both *cat* and *bat*. Write the word *bat* on the chart paper and ask children to read the word again.

Next, write *-at* above the word *cat* and tell the class that they are going to figure out more words that belong to the *-at* word family. Ask children to think of other letters they could put in front of *-at* to make new words. With each suggestion that makes a real word, add the first letter to the magnetic -*at* and write the word on the chart paper.

Explain to children that, as a group, they will be working on lots of different word families in the coming weeks, and that, independently, they can choose to work on word families. Show children where magnetic letters, magnet boards, and special paper for recording word families are stored.

Supporting Children's Learning

When a class begins focusing on word families, there will always be some children who do not yet hear—or recognize—the rhyming nature of words in word families. It is usually a matter of time and experience. Continue offering these children opportunities to listen to books, poems, and songs that feature rhyming words and discussing the words that rhyme.

Expanding the Lesson

There are 37 phonograms recommended by reading research as the most important to teach young children. Children can read and spell more than 500 words using: -ack, -ail, -ain, -ake, -ale, -ame, -an, -ank, -ap, -ash, -at, -ate, -aw, -ay, -eat, -ell, -est, -ice, -ick, -ide, -ight, -ill, -in, -ine, -ing, -ink, -ip, -it, -ock, -oke, -op, -or, -ore, -uck, -ug, -ump, and -unk.

1W **2F**

Creating Sentences in a Pocket Chart

Lesson Target

To reinforce the concept that sentences consist of several words

Why Teach This

It is not easy for young children to learn exactly what a sentence is. Once young children start writing, a sentence can go on and on. They need to work with many, many sentences before they internalize that a sentence must contain a noun and a verb and consist of one thought. Manipulating words in pocket charts helps make this concept less abstract.

Secondary Objective

- To reinforce appropriate word order for English sentences

Links to ELA Standards

- Students read a wide range of print and nonprint texts to build an understanding of texts.
- Students apply knowledge of language structure and language conventions to discuss print texts.

Learning Materials
- sentence strips
- markers
- scissors
- pocket chart

Time Range
15–20 minutes

Before You Start
Hang the pocket chart at a level where children can reach all pockets. Choose the sentences to use in this introductory lesson. The best choices are beginning sentences from a familiar children's books or some of the children's dictated sentences from a recent "News of the Day" (see page 90). Select three or four short sentences. Write one sentence on a sentence strip and copy it again on a second strip. Write each of the other sentences on a sentence strip. Copy each sentence on a second strip, then cut it apart into individual words.

Students' Prior Experience
Children have learned other individual routines that are done in partners.

To Do
Gather children in the group meeting area so they can all see the pocket chart. Explain that in this lesson, you will be reading a sentence, then taking it apart into its individual words. Display two sentence strips with the same sentence written on each one. Ask children to read the sentence together as you point to the words. Make sure they notice the two sentences are the same.

Point out that this sentence tells a complete thought. You might point out the *who* (subject) and the *what they did* (predicate) parts of the sentence. Ask children to reread the sentence. Put one of the strips in the pocket chart.

Direct children's attention to the other sentence strip as you cut the words apart. Place the individual words in order in the pocket chart as you cut them apart. Reread the sentence. Remove the individual words, mixing them up. Then place them back in order.

Distribute the word cards to children, asking them to work together to re-create the sentence. Have them reread the sentence after they are finished. Remind children that sentences use words to tell a complete thought.

Supporting Children's Learning
Make a game of this lesson to support English-language learners and less-capable children. Write two or three sentences on sentence strips. Read the sentences to the group, then have the children read the sentences with you. Cut the words apart in front of the group, then put the words back into the pocket chart in order. Choose one child to be "it." Everyone else closes their eyes while "it" turns over one word in the sentence. At a signal, everyone opens their eyes and reads the sentences to him- or herself and tries to identify the hidden word.

ⓌW ②F
Creating Story Maps

Lesson Target

To give children visual support to guide their thinking/comprehension when they are reading a story

Why Teach This

Children with different learning styles need different kinds of support to enhance their comprehension of what they read. Graphic organizers, such as story maps, help visual learners focus on individual features of fiction stories. Having the story map in front of them as they read helps children pay closer attention to features such as the names of characters, the setting, and so on.

Secondary Objective

- To help children develop a sense of story structure

Links to ELA Standards

- Students read a wide range of print and nonprint texts to build an understanding of texts.
- Students participate as knowledgeable, reflective, creative, critical members of a variety of literacy communities.

Learning Materials

- familiar children's book, such as *Goldilocks and the Three Bears*
- transparency of "Story Map I" (page 107)
- dry-erase or transparency markers
- overhead projector
- copies of "Story Map I" for each child

Time Range

15–20 minutes

Before You Start

Prepare a transparency of "Story Map I." Select a familiar children's book that has an obvious setting, strong characters, and a clear beginning, middle, and end (for example, *Goldilocks and the Three Bears*).

Students' Prior Experience

Children should be familiar with group routines, listening carefully to read-alouds, and discussing story characteristics (plot, setting, characters) they have heard.

To Do

Gather children in the group meeting area, making sure everyone can see the screen for the overhead projector. Explain that you will be reading a story and that when you're finished, you will fill a story map of the book. Explain that a "story map" is a special type of graphic organizer that is used to record information about stories. Read *Goldilocks and the Three Bears* (or another book with similar characteristics).

Ask children: *What is the setting for this book?* If necessary, define *setting*—the time when and place where a story takes place. When children answer, place the "Story Map I" transparency on the overhead projector. Write *the forest* beside the word "Setting." Invite the class to list the characters in this story. As children name *Goldilocks, Father Bear, Mother Bear,* and *Baby Bear,* fill in these words beside "Characters."

Ask the class: *What happened at the very beginning of this story?* If children do not respond fairly quickly, turn to the first page of the story and show the illustrations to the class. Fill in the "Beginning" section of the story map with children's comments.

Next, ask: *What happened at the very end of this story?* If necessary, turn to the last page of the story and show the illustrations to the class. Fill in the "Ending" section of the story map with children's comments.

Then ask the class: *What are some of the things that happened in the middle of this story?* Turn to the second page of the story, showing the illustrations to the class and turning the pages slowly. Fill in the "Middle" section of the story map with children's comments. When the story map is complete, read it aloud. After children have had several experiences creating story maps as a class, challenge groups of four to six students to work collaboratively to produce story maps. Finally, after multiple experiences, ask children to generate story maps on their own.

Supporting Children's Learning

If some children have difficulty focusing on all components of a story map, reduce the number of components children identify. Working with small groups over a week's time, read simple stories and have children list the characters in each story. The next week, reread the same stories, this time having children discuss the stories' settings, and so on.

Expanding the Lesson

Before asking children to complete graphic organizers such as story maps, model working through the format several times with the whole class. Then have children work on story maps in small groups. After multiple experiences using Story Map I (page 107), consider introducing a similar graphic organizer (see page 108).

Story Map I

Story Title _____

Setting _____

Characters _____

Beginning

Middle

Ending

Story Map II

Story Title _____

What is the problem in this story?

_____

_____

_____

_____

What important things happened in the story?

_____

_____

_____

_____

How is the problem solved?

_____

_____

_____

_____

1W **2F**

Rereading Familiar Stories

Lesson Target
To increase children's fluency

Why Teach This
The single best way for children to increase their reading fluency is to reread familiar stories; however, this is not a reading choice that most young children choose. Offering unique or novel ways to read often entices children into rereading familiar stories. This lesson offers one such suggestion.

Secondary Objective
• To give students a reason to choose to reread stories

Links to ELA Standards
• Students read a wide range of print and nonprint texts to build an understanding of texts.
• Students apply a wide range of strategies to comprehend, interpret, evaluate, and appreciate texts.

Learning Materials
• several books at different reading levels
• 5 or 6 whisper telephones (see "Teacher Tip" below)
• spray disinfectant (or other cleaning agent)

Time Range
10–15 minutes

Before You Start
Gather at least four to six whisper telephones so everyone in a small group can practice using the "telephone." Collect 12 to 18 books that represent the different reading levels of children in the class. Select one short book to read during the lesson as a model.

Teacher Tip
Whisper telephones can be purchased commercially or made using two small pieces of PVC pipe connected by a PVC joint.

Students' Prior Experience

Children have read aloud to the teacher and to a partner several times.

To Do

Gather children in the group meeting area. Explain to the class that you are introducing a new activity for reading-choice time. Show a whisper phone to the class and ask: *What do you think this is? What do you think you would use it for?* After listening to children's predictions, explain: *This little piece of pipe works almost like magic. When someone talks into one end of it, the voice is* amplified, *which means, made louder.*

Read two or three pages from a book, using a very soft voice. Explain to children that this is as loud as anyone using the whisper phone needs to read. Demonstrate how to clean the telephone after use. Show children where the whisper telephones and cleaning agent will be kept.

Explain that all children will get a chance to try out a whisper telephone sometime during today's reading-choice time, and that you will call children when it is their turn. Call on four to six children to stay in the group meeting area to experiment with the telephones. Dismiss other children to reading-choice time.

Supporting Children's Learning

Some children tend to play around with the telephones when first introduced to them. Usually children get more serious when the teacher moves closer to them. Close proximity to children who are being silly often solves that problem without conversation or reminders about behavior.

◄ Expanding the Lesson ►

Another way to entice children into rereading familiar stories is to have them audiotape themselves when they can read a story "just like" the people who create the books on tape. When children know that these tapes will be placed in the listening center and that classmates can choose those tapes to listen to, many children become motivated to practice reading a book until they are "good enough" to record.

CHAPTER FOUR

For Independent Readers

Overview

Kindergarten through second-grade independent readers are children who have deciphered the "code" of reading; that is, they have figured out that letters have sounds and that these sounds go together to form words. They also know that these words, separated by spaces and combined with other words, result in a complete thought. They no longer memorize texts and pretend to "read" them aloud. They need less support than early readers but are not skilled enough to read completely on their own.

Independent readers see how to group letters together and how to divide words into syllables. They know that -*tion* is the sound at the end of *vacation* and do not individually sound out each letter. They are not stymied by the /a/ sound in *eight* or the silent letters involved with the /igh/ sound in *light*.

These independent readers are anxious to learn the secrets that reading allows them to know. Since their focus is not on the mechanics of reading, they are free to concentrate on fluency and begin to realize how stories go together. A new interest in informational text and longer fiction books results. These children like to learn about sharks or dinosaurs, proudly telling others the facts they have learned. They get hooked on series books, reading the *Magic Tree House* books by Mary Pope Osborne or other chapter books, like those by Judy Blume. They begin to expect to see particular features in their reading.

The routines and activities for independent readers focus on lessons that build on these skills. Learning to ask questions, find answers, critique a story, or make an inference are skills that these children are ready to learn.

Checklist of Signs of Independent Readers

☐ **1.** Child wants to read to others often.

☐ **2.** Child recognizes many common sight words.

☐ **3.** Child consistently uses multiple reading strategies to read unknown words.

☐ **4.** Child comprehends story for books at his or her reading level.

☐ **5.** Child reads orally with meaning and expression.

Strategies for Independent Readers

1S **2W**

Asking Questions and Finding Answers

Lesson Target
To help students learn to recognize answers in expository text to student-posed questions

Why Teach This
Young children typically ask a lot of questions, but rarely see themselves as capable of answering those questions. This lesson would be the first of many opportunities children need to pose questions then look for resources where they can find the answers. This type of learning experience is the first step of teaching research skills.

Secondary Objective
• To help children ask questions related to one topic

Links to ELA Standards
• Students gather, evaluate, and synthesize data from a variety of sources.
• Students use a variety of technological and informational resources to gather and synthesize information and to create and communicate knowledge.
• Students employ a wide range of strategies as they write and use different writing process elements appropriately to communicate with different audiences.

Learning Materials
• at least one nonfiction book related to gardening (or any other topic) for every two children in the class (see sidebar at right for suggestions)

For the topic of gardening, expository texts might include:

From Acorn to Oak Tree by Jan Kottke (Children's Press, 2000)

From Seed to Dandelion by Jan Kottke (Children's Press, 2000)

From Seed to Plant by Gail Gibbons (Holiday House, 1993)

From Seed to Sunflower by Gerald Legg (Franklin Watts, 1998)

Fruit Is a Suitcase for Seeds by Jean Richards (Millbrook Press, 2002)

How a Seed Grows by Helene J. Jordan (HarperTrophy, 1992)

It's a Fruit, It's a Vegetable, It's a Pumpkin by Allan Fowler (Children's Press, 1996)

Jack's Garden by Henry Cole (HarperTrophy, 1997)

The Magic School Bus Plants Seeds: A Book About How Living Things Grow by Joanna Cole (Scholastic, 1995)

One Bean by Anne F. Rockwell (Walker & Co., 1999)

Pumpkin Circle: The Story of a Garden by George Levenson (Tricycle Press, 2002)

Pumpkin Pumpkin by Jeanne Titherington (HarperTrophy, 1990)

The Reason for a Flower by Ruth Heller (Putnam, 1999)

A Seed Grows: My First Look at a Plant's Life Cycle by Pamela Hickman (Kids Can Press, 1997)

A Seed Is a Promise by Claire Merrill (Scholastic, 1990)

- basket large enough to hold all these books
- posterboard labeled "Questions About Gardening"
- 2 extra posterboards (in case children pose too many questions)
- glue stick
- 4-by-6-inch index cards (for children's questions)
- 4-by-6-inch index cards in a different color (for children's answers)
- small basket or tray to hold completed answer cards
- concrete objects related to the topic that might prompt children to pose questions

Time Range
30–45 minutes

Before You Start
Gather a sufficient number of nonfiction books related to gardening, or any other topic you decide to cover. Bring in objects related to the topic, such as seeds, small plantings, trowels, rakes, and hoes.

Students' Prior Experience
Children have had many experiences posing questions about one topic.

To Do
Gather children in the group meeting area and ask them to sit in a large circle. Place the garden-related objects in the center of the circle. Ask: *What do all these objects have in common?* When children point out that all the items are related to plants or gardening, explain that the class will be learning about gardening and maybe even plant their own garden.

Expanding the Lesson
This experience is much more effective if you follow through by having the class actually plant a garden. Children are much more interested in asking and answering questions about any topic if they really need to know that information to accomplish something that they want to do. The garden need not be large. A small section of the playground is sufficient to create a class garden. Likewise, seeds could be planted in large barrels just outside the doors of the building.

Ask: *What would we need to learn if we were going to plant our own garden?* When children begin responding with questions, say: *Wait a minute. I think we need to record these questions.* Get the index cards you've designated for questions and write children's questions on them, one question per card. Show children the posterboard labeled "Questions About Gardening." Reread children's questions, gluing each question card to the posterboard as you read it. (Make sure to leave enough room between cards so that an answer card can be posted next to its question card).

Explain to the class that most questions can be answered by reading books. Say that you have gathered many books about plants and gardening. Ask children to find a partner, select a book together, and begin to look for answers to the posed questions.

Show children the colored index cards for answers and ask them to write the answers they find on each of the cards. Indicate the basket you have prepared to hold the completed answer cards. Tell children to put each card in the basket after they have written an answer on it. Dismiss children a few at a time to get a book and begin looking for answers.

At a later meeting, take out the answer cards and read the answers aloud one at a time. With the class, determine which question the card answers, then glue the answer card beside its corresponding question.

Reread the questions that have not been answered. Give children a second block of time to look for answers. Then read these answers and post them beside the correct question.

Supporting Children's Learning

Some children may have difficulty keeping track of all the questions that are posed as they search expository texts for answers. Narrow down the number of questions these children are searching for to one or two. Make sure these questions are phrased simply and can be easily located. Provide specific books for struggling children to use.

Expanding the Lesson

Children will probably not find answers to all of their questions during the first block of research time. The fact that their reading levels are still emerging also limits them. Even if you read parts of the books aloud to answer children's questions, there may still be questions that remain unanswered. Children's books may not have all the answers the children are seeking. This is a good time to show children how to consult with experts to answer questions they cannot answer themselves. Find a parent or grandparent in the school who has an avid interest in gardening and invite him to the classroom to act as the expert for the class's questions.

1S 2F
Making Inferences

Lesson Target

To help children learn to use information in a text to draw a conclusion that is implied but not specifically mentioned in the story or book

Why Teach This

Making inferences goes beyond the literal meaning of a book to understanding what the author implied through his or her words. Skillful, insightful readers make inferences about how a character feels even though the author does not directly describe the character's feelings. Good readers figure out how events affect characters even though these issues were not discussed specifically.

Young children are quite concrete in their thinking. Making inferences requires abstract thinking, so most young children will need to be guided in this area many times before you can expect them to make inferences independently.

Secondary Objective

• To apply this ability to infer to events that occur in children's lives, helping them learn to evaluate situations and make appropriate responses or decisions

Links to ELA Standards

- Students apply a wide range of strategies to comprehend, interpret, evaluate, and appreciate texts.
- Students participate as knowledgeable, reflective, creative, critical members of a variety of literacy communities.

Learning Material

- poem or book that uses inferences

Time Range

20–25 minutes

Before You Start

Find a poem or book that will interest the class and that lends itself to making inferences; for example, the poem "New Kid on the Block" by Jack Prelutsky or the book *White Dynamite and Curly Kid* by Bill Martin, Jr. (Henry Holt, 1989).

Students' Prior Experience

Children have had multiple experiences predicting the end of a story or the next event in a story or book.

To Do

Gather children in the group meeting area.

Read the poem "New Kid on the Block" by Jack Prelutsky. In this poem, the "new kid" does mean things to everyone. The reader assumes that the "new kid" is a boy but the last verse reveals her as a girl.

Ask children: *Were you surprised to find out that the new kid is a girl? What details of the poem led you to believe the character was a boy?* Explain that readers often "make inferences," or draw conclusions about a story even though the author doesn't say something directly. Suggest that good readers look at all the details and make inferences about the text after carefully considering all the details.

At another session, read *White Dynamite and Curly Kid.* Just like with the poem, readers assume that the child in this book is a boy, but it turns out to be a girl. Remind children of the strategies of looking at all the details before making inferences.

Supporting Children's Learning

Real-life experiences with making inferences are the best way to fine-tune this skill. When children have a question about an event or happening, turn that question back to them to answer. Ask: *Why do you think that?* Or, *If _____ happens, then what will be the result?* Often a teacher's first impulse is to provide children with the answers they seek; but if you lead them to discover the answer themselves, children learn a more meaningful lesson.

TEACHING STRATEGIES

Questions that lead children into making inferences include:

- What did (a particular event in the story) make you think about?
- What did the ending of the story make you think about?
- What do you think this character really meant by saying that?
- Why did this character (act, think, talk) that way?
- How do you think this character felt when (a particular event in the story) happened?
- What is this story really about?
- What does this character want to do?
- What do you think this character might do?
- What is the author really trying to say?

Strategies list adapted from Fountas & Pinnell, 2001

1S 2F

Reading With Expression

Lesson Target
To help children learn to read aloud with expression

Why Teach This
Even though you may regularly model expressive reading, children do not always translate this to their own reading. Opportunities such as this lesson help children make connections between your expressive reading and their own.

Secondary Objective
- To make explicit the reading strategies that children need to use in their independent reading

Link to ELA Standards
- Students apply knowledge of language structure and language conventions to discuss print texts.

Learning Materials
- novel that has quite a bit of dialogue between the same characters
- transparencies
- overhead projector
- highlighters, at least two colors

Time Range
10–15 minutes

Before You Start
To model using different voices for each character, select a novel with a limited number of characters that has dialogue. *Frog and Toad All Year* by Arnold Lobel (HarperCollins, 1984) has simple enough text for children to read easily while offering the contrasts of Frog and Toad's personalities. *George and Martha* by James Marshall (Houghton Mifflin, 1974) also uses clear dialogue between the two characters.

   Make overhead transparencies of the pages you will read and highlight the two characters' words in contrasting colors.

Students' Prior Experience
Children have had many experiences listening to you read using different voices for different characters.

To Do
Gather children in the group meeting area and have them sit so everyone can see the screen for the overhead projector. Begin by saying something like: *I always read with*

expression but realized that I have not shown you how I know what expressions to use.

Display the first transparency of the pages you intend to read. Point out that Frog's words are highlighted in one color and Toad's words are highlighted in a different color. As you begin to read, exaggerate the voice you use for each character. For example, make Toad speak in a deep voice while Frog's voice is pitched higher. Adapt your intonations to the words and their meaning, e.g., when a character gets excited, read his part faster and in an excited voice.

At the end of the story, ask children what they noticed about the way you read. Lead them to understand that you followed the author's suggestions and made your voice match the text. For example, if the author wrote that the character "bellowed" or "whispered" you would adjust your voice accordingly.

Teacher Tip

Hold an index card under the text you want children to focus on. Move the card down the page as you read. You can also cut a frame from an index card and use that to focus children's attention on a particular part of the text.

Supporting Children's Learning

Most children benefit from practice with this skill. Assign children partners, provide them with copies of the text, and ask them to take turns reading the different parts.

Children who have trouble following this lesson on the overhead may benefit from having the text in their own hand. Distribute highlighted photocopies of the text before you begin to read from the transparency.

Expanding the Lesson

Make a simple mask to hold while you read the different parts. Color the masks to look like the characters in the story. Attach the masks to tongue depressors and hold them up as you read the parts. This helps visual learners connect the expressive voice they hear with the characters' faces they see.

1S **2F**

Reviewing Self-Monitoring Strategies

Lesson Target

To support children's independent monitoring of their own reading comprehension

Why Teach This

Some children subconsciously monitor their comprehension of text. Other children, however, may recognize when something does not make sense but do not know what to do at this point. Outlining the actions readers take when they do not understand what they read helps build children's comprehension.

Secondary Objective

- To increase fluency by aiding comprehension

Link to ELA Standards

- Students apply a wide range of strategies to comprehend, interpret, evaluate, and appreciate texts.

Learning Materials

- chart tablet
- felt-tip markers

Time Range

15–20 minutes

Before You Start

Choose a paragraph with a reading level that is slightly above the independent reading level of most students. Copy the paragraph onto chart paper.

Students' Prior Experience

Most children are at the independent reading stage.

To Do

Gather children in the group meeting area. Explain that good readers notice when they do not understand what they are reading or when something does not make sense, and they do something about it. Ask children: *Have you ever read something that you don't understand or doesn't make sense? What do you do when this happens to you?*

Write children's comments on chart paper. Lead children to mention the following strategies:

- Stop and think about what you've read.
- Keep on reading and see if that helps.
- Go back and read the sentence or paragraph again.
- Ask for help during a reading conference.
- Ask a friend sitting close by.

Read aloud the paragraph you prepared and model using the strategies listed above.

Supporting Children's Learning

If children have trouble using all five strategies, work with them one-on-one or in small groups, emphasizing one strategy at a time.

Whole- and Small-Group Reading Activity

1S **2F**

Participating in Book Talks

Lesson Target

To support children's ability to summarize and critique books they have read independently

Why Teach This

Book talks are a great way to introduce children to new books and to spark their interest in reading these books. Book talks help children gain a deeper understanding of the text, teaching them about parts of a story, conflict and resolution, rising and falling action, and so on. Model book talks before expecting children to present their own book talks.

Secondary Objective

• To support children's ability to speak in front of the class

Link to ELA Standards

• Students participate as knowledgeable, reflective, creative, critical members of a variety of literacy communities.

Learning Material

• book at the group's reading level

Time Range

5–10 minutes

Before You Start

Select text appropriate to the group you are working with and prepare a book talk as if you are writing a commercial for the book.

Students' Prior Experience

Children have read a wide variety of books, written summaries and book reviews, and listened to a teacher model book talks.

To Do

Gather children in the group meeting area. Begin by saying something like: *By now, all of you have read several books and can probably talk a little bit about them—for example, say what the story is about and whether or not you liked it. Today, I am going to model for you how to do a "book talk."*

Take the book you selected and show the children its front cover. Tell them the title, author, and illustrator (if there is one). Read aloud the first paragraph or another equally interesting paragraph, so children get a feel for the author's style of writing. Then give a brief summary of the book. Connect the book to another book the children know well—and perhaps connect the book to the children's lives. Critique the book, sharing your personal response to the book.

Explain to children that you will be inviting them to do a book talk within the next few days.

Supporting Children's Learning

If children are hesitant to give a book talk to the entire class, suggest that they write a script, as if they were writing a commercial, then videotape their book talk.

Individual & Partner Reading Activities

1S **2F**

Writing Summaries

Lesson Target

To understand the components of a good summary

Why Teach This

One of the first comprehension strategies that children learn is summarizing a book. Many children find this skill difficult, however. They tend to either retell the story in detail or are not sure where to begin. They are stymied when they try to recall various events in the story, often losing their place in their summarization. Summarizing involves not only remembering important events in the story or book, but also describing them in a concise way. Children need to have this skill modeled for them and be involved in creating summaries in groups before they are asked to do this independently.

Secondary Objectives

- To identify important information while children are reading
- To distinguish between summarizing important information and retelling all details of a story or book

Link to ELA Standards

- Students apply a wide range of strategies to comprehend, interpret, evaluate, and appreciate texts.

Learning Materials

- piece of quality children's literature (for example, Tomie dePaola's *Strega Nona*)
- chart tablet
- several colored markers

- transparency of professionally written summary of selected book (see "Teacher Tip" at right)
- blank transparency
- dry-erase or transparency pen
- overhead projector

Time Range

20–30 minutes

Before You Start

Find a book that children are already familiar with and that has obvious events children can list. A good example is *Strega Nona* by Tomie dePaola (Simon & Schuster, 1975).

Students' Prior Experience

Children have had multiple experiences listening to stories and being involved in discussions about those stories. They have been involved in many oral and written demonstrations of good summaries.

To Do

Gather children in the group meeting area. Tell children that today the class will write the summary of a book. Explain that a summary is a short description of what happens in the book.

Read *Strega Nona* to the class. Ask children to think back to the beginning of the story and tell what happened first. Write children's comments on chart paper.

Ask: *What happened next?* Record their answers.

Continue asking: *What happened next?* until children have identified the important events in the story. If children skip an

Teacher Tip

Accessing Internet sites is a quick way to find summaries of familiar books. Amazon.com and bn.com provide brief descriptions of books. For example, the description for *Strega Nona* on Amazon.com is:

Strega Nona—"Grandma Witch"—is the source for potions, cures, magic, and comfort in her Calabrian town. Her magical ever full pasta pot is especially intriguing to hungry Big Anthony. He is supposed to look after her house and tend her garden, but one day, when she goes over the mountain to visit Strega Amelia, Big Anthony recites the magic verse over the pasta pot, with disastrous results.

TEACHING STRATEGIES

Other Strategies to Practice Summarizing

- Write a summary yourself of a book that is familiar to all children in the class. Then ask children to examine the example and identify characteristics that make it a good summary (see page 122).

- Use short books—with only a few major events—that are easier to summarize.

- Have heterogeneous groups of children work together to write summaries.

- Have each child write a summary. Then have children work in pairs to revise each person's summary, making them more concise.

- Have children write a summary of a book after they have presented it in a book talk.

- Have children try to write a summary of a book after having heard about it from a book talk.

important event, write down the comment anyway, then ask if anything happened between the last two events written on the chart paper. For example: *Did anything important happen between the time that Strega Nona went to visit Strega Amelia and when the pasta began to bubble out of the magic pot?*

When all major events have been noted, ask children to think about which three events are most important to getting the gist of the story. Encourage children to discuss in pairs, identify what they think are the three most important events, and be prepared to say why they think that. Give pairs three or four minutes for their discussion.

Ask one pair to share what they discussed. On chart paper, write a brief summary based on their three events. Read the summary aloud.

Next, put a transparency of a professionally written summary of the same book on the overhead. Ask children which summary is better and why. Invite them to identify some of the characteristics of a good summary. Write their comments on the chart tablet. Some characteristics children may mention include:

- tells who the main characters are;
- tells where the story happens;
- starts at the beginning of the story;
- tells important events in order;
- tells how the story ends.

Explain that children will write their own summaries from time to time in the next few days.

Supporting Children's Learning

Children will need many opportunities to become good at writing summaries. If, after writing several summaries, children are still struggling, work with them one-on-one.

25

Reading the Newspaper

Lesson Target

To give students strategies for reading the newspaper genre

Why Teach This

Reading expository texts requires different reading strategies than reading fiction stories. Help children learn these strategies by explaining the strategies, modeling how they are implemented, and providing multiple opportunities for children to practice using them.

Secondary Objective

- To extend children's strategies for reading expository text

Links to ELA Standards

- Students read a wide range of print and nonprint texts to build an understanding of texts.
- Students apply a wide range of strategies to comprehend, interpret, evaluate, and appreciate texts.
- Students use a variety of technological and informational resources to gather and synthesize information and to create and communicate knowledge.

Learning Materials

- copies of the same short newspaper article for each child
- highlighters for each child
- transparency of the article
- dry-erase or transparency pens
- overhead projector
- more short, high-interest newspaper articles

Time Range

15–20 minutes

Before You Start

Find a short newspaper article that would interest most children in your class. Make sure that the five W's (*who, what, when, where,* and *why*) in the article are easily identifiable. Make an overhead transparency of the article and photocopies for children. Clip more short, high-interest articles for your reading center.

Students' Prior Experience

Children have had multiple experiences reading informational texts.

To Do

Gather children in the group meeting area and have them sit so everyone

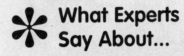

What Experts Say About...

Strategies That Readers Need When Processing Informational Text

- Establish a clear purpose for reading.
- Make connections with prior knowledge and experience.
- Integrate cues from written and visual text.
- Summarize information.
- Analyze and synthesize information.
- Notice and interpret text structures.
- Question the author and the text.
- Use organizational features quickly and efficiently.

Source: Hoyt, Mooney, & Parkes (2003)

can see the screen for the overhead projector. Distribute the photocopied article and ask children to read it silently. Display the transparency of the article on the overhead projector.

Ask children: *Where do you think I got the article?* If they do not immediately recognize this as an article from a newspaper, give sufficient clues until someone guesses *newspaper*. Show the class the page from the newspaper that contains the article.

Explain that newspaper articles usually have distinct features: The important details about the topic are given in the first couple of sentences, and journalists tell the *who*, *what*, *when*, *where*, and *why* of the topic. Have children reread the article to find the "who" in the article, highlight it, and write the word *who* next to that line in the article. Ask one child to read the words that she highlighted. Underline those words on the transparency.

Next, have children reread the article to find the "what" in the article, highlight it, and write the word *what* next to that line in the article. Ask one child to read the words that he highlighted, and underline those words on the transparency. Continue the same procedure with *when*, *where*, and *why*.

Explain that copies of different articles will be available in the reading center for children to practice reading newspaper articles and recognizing the five W's.

Supporting Children's Learning

Work one-on-one with children who have difficulty locating different parts of a newspaper article. Sometimes newspaper articles are intimidating for young children. Beginning with informational articles from magazines or newspapers designed for children can be helpful.

> ### Expanding the Lesson
>
> One of the best ways to reinforce how to analyze a newspaper article is to have children create their own articles, using real newspaper articles as models. Consider having children choose different topics and create a class newspaper.

2S

Writing Book Reviews

Lesson Target

To help children write summaries and critiques of books they have read on their own

Why Teach This

Book reviews give teachers insight into a child's comprehension and his ability to write summaries or critiques of books. Readers make judgments about books while reading them. Sometimes the judgment is to stop reading the book because, perhaps, the reader finds it boring, silly, or too difficult. Sometimes children judge a book as "really good." But too often children's evaluation does not

go further than "I liked this book," or "I did not like this book." Children become more purposeful in their judgments when they have to support their surface judgments with reasons. Writing book reviews helps develop this skill.

Secondary Objectives

- To critique books/stories
- To give reasons supporting why children like or dislike a book

Links to ELA Standards

- Students employ a wide range of strategies as they write and use different writing process elements appropriately to communicate with different audiences.
- Students apply a wide range of strategies to comprehend, interpret, evaluate, and appreciate texts.
- Students participate as knowledgeable, reflective, creative, critical members of a variety of literacy communities.

Learning Materials

- one or two book reviews of books familiar to the class
- transparency of each review
- one short book familiar to everyone in the class
- blank transparencies
- dry-erase or transparency pens
- overhead projector

Time Range

15–20 minutes

Before You Start

Locate professional reviews of books that are familiar to students in the class. You'll find appropriate book reviews in journals such as *Horn Book, Bulletin of the Center for Children's Books, Preview, Language Arts,* and *Reading Teacher.*

Students' Prior Experience

Children have written several summaries of books.

To Do

Gather children in the group meeting area. Explain to children that you will be looking at some reviews of books that they're familiar with. Display transparencies of professionally written book reviews on the overhead projector. Read them aloud.

Ask children to identify features of a book review, guiding them to list such things as:

- states title, author, and illustrator;
- briefly tells what the book is about;
- presents opinions about the book;

Teacher Tip

Note that writing a review of a book is different from writing a summary of a book. A review calls for making judgments about the book and expressing personal opinions about it. Reviewers sometimes contrast the book with previous ones by the same author or make other comparisons. Books are recommended (or not) in a review. A summary does not include evaluative statements.

Expanding the Lesson

Most adults remember the negative experience of being required to write book reports in elementary school. Book reviews are not standard book reports. Photocopy book reviews from journals or newspapers, and post them on a "Book Reviews" bulletin board as models for children. Add children's reviews to this bulletin board. Having an audience for book reviews that they have written makes a difference in children's attitudes about writing them.

You might also consider producing a catalog of book reviews; for instance, ask children to read a Tomie dePaola book and write a review of it. Collect all children's reviews and publish them in a catalog to be given to other classes at the same grade level and to the school library.

- relates book to other titles; and
- highlights special things about the book.

Explain to children that they will work together to write a book review today. Read aloud a short book. Lead a class discussion to review this book, using the features identified above. Write children's remarks on a transparency. Wrap up the discussion by asking if they would recommend this book to other children. Write their answers.

Read this book review aloud, asking the class if they need to add anything else to the review. Explain that you will be asking them to write their own reviews from time to time in the next few days.

Supporting Children's Learning

Have children work in small heterogeneous groups to write reviews of familiar books together. This will support children who find writing book reviews challenging.

25

Taping, Checking, and Charting

Lesson Target

To increase children's reading fluency

Why Teach This

The target of many reading lessons is to increase fluency. We want children to read more and understand better. By introducing a variety of ways to practice this skill, you increase the opportunities in the classroom for successful reading experiences.

Secondary Objectives

- To help children learn to monitor their own reading
- To reinforce reading strategies for decoding unknown words

Links to ELA Standards

- Students apply a wide range of strategies to comprehend, interpret, evaluate, and appreciate texts.
- Students use spoken and written language to accomplish their own purposes.

Learning Materials

- handheld tape recorder
- blank audiotape
- short book
- transparencies of the book's pages
- photocopies of other short books children may want to read
- 3 colors of markers or pens
- overhead projector